Planetary Ascension:
The Purpose of 3D
and the Choice We Face

"Maria Owl is a beacon of light in these challenging dark times. In this powerful book, she brings light into the heart of darkness and illuminates that which has been controlling humanity for eons. She also, with the help of the higher beings she channels, shares the profound wisdom that it is love that opens the doors to ascension to us, and that journey can only happen within each one of us."   Dr. Melissa Sophia Joy, Founder of Somatic Awakening®

"I believe the book "Planetary Ascension: The Purpose of 3D and The Choice We Face" is a significant and important book for our current times of challenge and chaos. Maria helps us see that these experiences are also times of great transformation and awakening on the planet. This book explains complex terms of the potential of our personal and collective evolution in simple ways, making what was perhaps intimidating, now easy to access. It's definitely the right book at the right time."   Debra Giusti, Author of Activate Your Soul Tribe

"Planetary Ascension is a practical guide for any of us who want to deeply understand, not only what is happening right now on the planet, our history and what's coming soon, but HOW TO use this information to truly awaken to Universal Love. I highly recommend this book for any soul desiring more depth and applicable instruction on how to choose love rather than fear within any circumstance."   Theresa Gutierrez Author and Founder of 11th Hour Shaman

"Maria's journey is powerful and the insights and wisdom she shares in these pages are what the world needs right now!"   Hydee Tehana, Author of What If...We Are Intergalactic Intelligence?

PLANETARY ASCENSION:

The Purpose of 3D and the Choice We Face

Cover Art by Lucinda Rae

ISBN# 978-1-7371722-0-8

Sacred Future

P.O. Box 4397

Kailua-Kona, Hawai'i

United States of America

I dedicate this book to the children of Tara.

Table of Contents

Channeled Transmissions

Table of Contents

Our planet is ascending. She is taking a quantum leap into her new form. She is feeding us her life force that we may join her. She is encouraging us to keep going.

INHALE...

Dear Fellow Wanderers,

This book literally began to pour forth from me over a few days in early January 2020, from the catalyst of reading The Ra Material: Law of One, Book IV[1]. I had hoped to publish my perspectives as a booklet of maybe thirty pages at the end of March of that year, but this goal was thwarted. In mid-March, my husband and I were on our way to Italy when the world suddenly shut down due to a virus spreading out of China. We flew home and I found myself consumed with research and lightwork-outreach. At the time of this writing, it is two years later - January, 2022 – and my booklet project has expanded to a book of 213 pages. The most incredible global upheaval has happened in the world in the last two years, (with more to come, I'm sure)! As someone who walks between the worlds I have perceived the larger planetary contexts of these times, while also living through them. It has been my intent through it all to inspire unity, faith, and the use of this catalytic time for awakening consciousness.

With this book I am desiring to share my broader spiritual context of these times with you, and the wonder and amazement that comes from that. Because some of this

---

[1] The Law of ONE, Book IV, by RA, an humble messenger of the Law of One: https://www.lawofone.info/, Credit to: www.llresearch.org

book was written at the start of the "global pandemic" and some written during and some at the collapse of it, you may experience different writing styles throughout, reflective of what stage I was living through.

Here is the original opening paragraph I wrote for this book in 2020, so you can also understand that previous inspiration:

In writing this book, I am attempting to tie together, in a comprehensive way, the information I've received about our planetary ascension process from the focused channeling sessions my husband Duane and I have been holding since 2016, along with the complementary information from the Law of One, Ra Material, brought through by L/L Research in the 1980's. I have also found many related reports of cosmic events recorded by NASA, as well as reports from insiders within the Disclosure Movement[2] which I found relevant.

I hope that if you are reading this, the transmission through which I received it is reaching you in its pure form. The information here is too important to be passed over. May it support your continued awakening and reconnection

---

[2] A movement of people who desire the full disclosure of the UFO phenomenon and extra-terrestrial contact with Earth into the public sphere.

to your true essential nature, and may you in turn be a catalyst for others.

Blessings,

Maria Christina Owl

Hawai'ian Islands

January 12, 2022

INTRODUCTION

What Is Ascension?

Before you begin reading, I want to invite you to release all previously held definitions of ascension. You may return to your ideas after reading this book, but for now, it will serve you more to have an open mind. Ascension, as a word, cannot hold the actual process and experience I'm referring to in this book. The English language is very linear and unintuitive. Yet, for my purposes of conveying my point and emphasizing the current important choice we face as a planet, I have chosen the word "ascension" as the most appropriate. Here is the definition offered by my MacBook dictionary:

as·cen·sion| əˈsen(t)SH(ə)n | noun [in singular]

• the act of rising to an important position or a higher level

• (Ascension) the ascent of Christ into heaven on the fortieth day after the Resurrection.

Now, building on this, I'm going to give you my definition of ascension, distilled from my own research and experiences over the decades, to orient you to the journey you're about to go on.

- Ascension is not an event, it is an awakening state of consciousness within each person. Just as DNA is encoded with instructions to create our specific cells, tissues, and organs during gestation, so too does our DNA have the instructions for ascension.[3]
- Ascension, like God, is ineffable, yet the experience of both is inevitable.
- Ascension is encoded into your physical, energetic and etheric blueprints. You are from and part of the Source who dreamed the constantly fractalling and spiraling becoming that is ascension.
- There are many levels of ascension, on small scales and larger scales, even grand cosmic scales.

I believe personal ascension is a journey inward, rather than outward. During many of my sessions with the Higher Dimensional Helpers, who I channel, I have been brought into a multi-dimensional state to experience first-hand how our bodies are portals. I have been shown the folly of the human belief that we travel out of the body at death, when we actually travel back home through the portal of our body. Some people prefer the term "inscension," instead of ascension, because of this inward focus. The ancient Tibetan Buddhist mystery practice of attaining the Rainbow Body at

---

[3] Research by Gregg Prescott, MS: https://in5d.com/proof-dna-upgrade/

the point of physical death is an example of our amazing ability to inscend. Photographic evidence shows Tibetan high lamas turning into a burst of light on their deathbeds and then phasing out of this reality, leaving no trace of their bodies behind. Personal ascension doesn't only look like this magnificent example though, it can also be experienced as illumination and insight into who and what you truly are, that changes your life forever.

The journey of ascension can be likened to being a conifer seed in a forest. The first phase of your life is completely focused on surviving; deepening your roots enough to send up your cotyledons and then first needles. It's all about you and your experience of growth. Every day is unknown. Will you have enough sunlight, water and nutrients to make it to be a sapling? But as your roots deepen over decades, you discover there is a vast network of roots connected together underground. You know this because your roots have intertwined with them instinctually, to share energy, nutrients and chemical information. You are not alone. Survival is not a private experience. Your self-identity expands to include the other trees around you, as well as the nutrients being taken up from the streams, the mycelial network, the bacteria, and the minerals. At the same time, your canopy grows higher and higher into the sky.

When before you were only aware of dappled light from the larger trees blocking your access to the sun, now you are tall and strong. Your branches are woven together with those of other trees, which supports you during a high wind or storm. You realize in your growing awareness that you needed the shade of the larger trees when you were a sapling to protect your tender new needles from the direct, hot sun. Gratitude for all these complex inner-connections swells in your heart! Your identity continues to expand to include the sunlight, rainfall, lightning and fire.

Whereas before you were tiny, now you are vast. You are aware that the forest, which you are an integral part of, spans for thousands of hectares in every direction, through valleys and up mountain sides. All of the roots of all of the trees are networked together, communicating. The older you get, the more you can participate in supporting the life of the forest – hosting fungi, mosses, lichens, birds, ferns, ants, and other insects on your body. You have an innate knowing that this growth will never end, it will continue on day after day, year after year, century after century, and you are continuously and delightfully surprised by the infinite creation within which you are embedded.

The beauty of this analogy is that even as a seed, the conifer was always part of the everything, it just didn't know it. We only understand who we are, based on what we believe is true, which often derives from what we observe. Our ability to observe grows stronger and wiser as we age, as people and as Souls. When we're young we perceive in basic ways and create stories to understand our world. Over time veils of illusion form and hide the truth from us. They are there to challenge and test us. As we develop, make mistakes, learn and grow, the veils drop. We inevitably graduate into greater and greater clarity and truth and we perceive reality more as it truly is.

As the Higher Dimensional Helpers told my partner Duane and I during one channeling session, "There are many levels of truth. We reveal to you what you are ready to hear. If we shared information with you beyond your ability to comprehend, you would reject it or suppress it, as if you never heard it. But if you take what we offer you and work with it, it becomes your own embodied wisdom, ripening you to receive the next level of truth."

To put it simply, personal ascension is our own journey of awakening to the truth of who and what we are, not just as people, but as Creators, and as Consciousness.

Now, what about Planetary Ascension? The Earth is our mother. She is a planet who is alive, conscious and evolving, and why wouldn't this be true? You are a person having a personal experience of thought forms and feelings; the Earth is a planet having a planetary experience of thought forms and feelings. These two things are inextricably linked. Your thoughts come from Earth, because you are part of Earth. As well, our planet is dreaming herself into her next experience constantly, and this frequency of her dreaming is constantly being transmitted through our bio-electric, watery, conduit bodies. Here's another way of describing it: *That which happens to our mother, we will experience on a personal level, and what we personally experience is absorbed into the greater planetary consciousness.*

Speaking of humanity being the children of Mother Earth, human beings are intrinsically connected to each other! Me with you. You with another. Them with others still. Everyone with each other. We are all wired like siblings who shared their mother's womb and have an uncanny ability to know each other's feelings and thoughts. You may have a notion that your thoughts are private, but what if they are a frequency being generated simultaneously by many around the world. For example, when you move towards healing, what if you are part of a greater wave of people making this choice to heal? You may be part of the initiation of this movement, courageously trailblazing through illusion and opening doors for others. Or you may be part of the tail end, resisting change until the movement has grown so strong is lifts you up and carries you through your fears, into transformation. Either way, we are all connected and impacted by each other's choices every moment of every day.

At this historical moment within our current timeline, we are moving through a graduation experience, from one level of awareness to the next higher level. Human consciousness is popping open, out of illusion and into the realization of our true nature. We are waking up to our true natures as divine human beings and the innate power that this gives us as reality-creators. This mass awakening will liberate our minds, hearts and Souls from the collective illusion and amnesia that have been part of this darker age we've been navigating through. Now, we are aligning at a rapid pace with the harmonic, natural order of our planet.

The Earth is transforming and taking a great evolutionary leap. You will discover as you read on how leaps like this have happened before and will happen again, like clockwork. And we are in the phase of the cycle now of birthing into a Golden Age on Earth!

CHAPTER 1

MY BACKGROUND AND LIFE AS A CHANNEL

How, you may be asking, has Maria Owl come to hold her current perspectives and inner-knowings about planetary ascension? Well, quite honestly, I'm asking this question myself! The simplest answer is, it has always interested me, more than any other inquiry. It is my passion to understand who we are, where we came from and where we're going. Deep in my heart, in quiet meditative moments, I'm filled with a knowing that I was born for this purpose in these times. The purpose is of being a catalyst for awakening. I think many of us feel this way, that we came to Earth now, specifically, to serve during this planetary upleveling. That this is the moment where humanity leaps into a new golden age of creativity, collaboration, and connection. But, serve how? Serve whom? Let's remember our conifer analogy. Once you've grown to a two-thousand-year-old Redwood tree, you have a perspective the newly germinated seeds in the ground don't have. Through shading them from direct sunlight, sharing nutrients through your roots, and inviting them into the awareness of inter-connection, you are serving those seeds.

Those on Earth who identify as *lightworkers* share a sense responsibility. We feel we've chosen to be born at this time of great change to support humanity in the awakening process. Our tools are patience, compassion, honesty, courage, determination, and especially love. Through these positive qualities and many more, we live as examples. Those who are ready to remember, find us.

I was born at home on November 3rd, 1972. I came through unexpectedly a month early, with a long hot bath to induce my arrival. I did not cry. My grandmother said when she first held me and looked into my eyes she knew I was a healer, like her father, the renown and beloved evangelical minister, Reverend Charles A. Shreve. And she was right. Though I spent my formative years trying to fit into the mainstream mold, pursuing marine biology and writing, I was destined to leave mainstream behind to fulfill my purpose.

Only looking back now can I map my path of initiation. Of course, while you're living it, it's just life, with its ups and downs, successes and failures, no different from anyone else. But, there are always unique weaves, twists and turns in everyone's life. The greater tapestry holding my smaller adventures reveals an epic journey. My life has been extra-ordinary, meaning, beyond what most people would call normal or ordinary. My perception, since birth, has always included other realms and invisible beings, both loving and terrifying. Fortunately, I never negated or denied my perceptions, or was made to by adults, though I rarely talked about what I perceived with anyone.

I've heard it said that old Souls choose childhood trauma to catalyze them onto their missions early. I don't know that this is true for everyone, but I feel it was for me. I don't want to divulge details of my past trauma in this book, but I do want you to understand that part of the celebration of my life today, is that I survived my childhood and I am now thriving. As soon as I was ready for initiation, and called for it, and the doors opened to me. I knew that if I didn't follow my Soul calling, my life would become unbearably difficult. My late teens and early twenties seemed to be one traumatic event after another. The suicides of dear friends, escalation of violence from my father, and stranger and stranger paranormal attacks against me. If I didn't head straight for the light, I felt I would be killed.

In 1994 I narrowly escaped death when my Toyota Four Runner spun out and flipped seven times on Interstate 80, after crossing the state line of Nevada into Utah. It was 2:00AM. I wasn't under the influence of anything. In fact, I was a big fan of sober living, coming from an alcoholic family. I wasn't sleepy. I was feeling wide awake as I excitedly drove to South Dakota to participate in my fourth Vision Quest. I was simply conversing with my friend. I turned my head for literally one second to look at him in the passenger seat, then looked back to the highway. For some unforeseen reason, my truck had turned and was driving out of our lane and into the soft, wide, center meridian. Fortunately, we were the only car on the road at that hour. I quickly responded, but didn't have the skill of driving in salt flats, my tires sunk in and we skid. The truck hopped back onto pavement with my frantic steering, but fish-tailed wildly until we flung into a roll. The realization came stark and clear into my mind, "I could die...".

To this day, I remember that moment vividly. There was no reason for the steering wheel to veer left. It was as if something else redirected the truck. Later I had a shamanic reading with a traditional medicine woman in Mexico. She saw that the negativity of the native medicine man I was learning from had grown very dark. This was true. The beings controlling him didn't want me to live. The following year when I finally did make it to the reservation to vision quest, he told me he knew why the accident happened, his guides had told him, but I wouldn't like it. He never told me what they'd said. All I know is that my friend and I stepped out of that crushed vehicle not only alive, but walking and conscious. I have no doubt that the Angels were surrounding and protecting us! I have no doubt that I am alive today because of their intervention, not just on that occasion, but on many, many occasions. This is just one example of how I dodged the attacks of negative beings who wanted to possess me, control me, or kill me.

After the accident I left mainstream education and entered onto the path of a holistic healer. I attained certifications in hypnotherapy, reiki, intuitive medicine and herbalism. In 2006 I went back to school for my Master's degree in Counseling Psychology. As well, I found myself deep diving into Indigenous wisdom and ceremony. I spent six years with that native teacher I mentioned above. Even after the accident, I continued to learn from him. In 1998, he crossed the line sexually with me for the last time, and I walked away for good. Parallel to all of this, at age 20, I was adopted into a Hopi family who believed in me and recognized my spiritual energy as a healer. They were my mirror of a healthy family, culture, and spiritual work.

Later, I studied earth-based healing from two African shamans from Burkina Faso, born into the Dagara tribe. Then at age 39, I initiated as a Priest of Yemoja in the Orisa religion, where I opened fully into my innate channeling and mediumship gift, but also met some very dark sorcerers. I studied with many other native elders and friends from many Indigenous cultures over the decades, including a very special man who became a dear friend, Lorin Smith of the Kashia Pomo tribe of California.

Shamanism was my language, my resonance, and my path. I believed it would protect me from the negative entities and people possessed by them, but sometimes it brought me into their lairs. One thing I've learned about spiritual initiations: as you become stronger, the tests get harder. Every disillusionment I faced, my discernment muscle grew. I came to perceive everyone as my mirror, helping me choose love over fear, truth over deception, who I am over what I'm not. My Higher Self tested me through testing my FAITH. That's the only muscle that really counts when the going gets tough.

Training as a Medium

In 2010 I had been praying for a final initiation with elders who could train me in mediumship and channeling, as no teacher before would approach this topic with me. Then my great test arrived! By invitation I entered into the most powerful shamanic training I'd ever encountered: the Ifa-Orisa traditions. This is a religion that traveled around the world, originating in Nigeria, Africa. The wisdom was pure. The elders I met, not so much. Orisa religion is what's called a spirit-possession tradition and those who practice it learn how to go into trance through singing praise songs and dancing to induce possession by spirit-entities, such as the loving Ancestors known as Egun, and the forces of nature known as Orisa. After dozens of rituals over three-years, I did indeed develop my mediumship and channeling ability within a community who weren't afraid of the gift, who knew how to create a powerful protected container for the process, and who could then help me interpret my experiences. If it had not been for the severe dysfunction within the community, I would have likely stayed. Yet, my

Higher Self and my new, strong connections to my elevated Orisa, guided me out and away from the whole religion.

One of the greatest gifts of my work with my head Orisa, Yemoja, who is identified as the Great Mother of Heavenly and Earthly Waters, an Ocean Goddess, and Protector of Children, was a deep cleansing of my heart. This Great Mother presence worked with me daily to forgive my past, forgive myself, and open to true love everywhere in my life. She brought me to the greatest love that I've ever known, and his name is Duane Michael.

Duane came on a wilderness rites of passage trip with me in the summer of 2012, by Labor Day weekend we were a thing. I introduced him into the Ifa-Orisa community and he chose to be initiated as well. We chose to sever from this community together in 2014. As crazy as things got in my life during that time, they became equally if not more beautiful and amazing afterward. I had made it through!

Where I was once fatigued, I now had vitality. Where I was once homeless, I now shared a beautiful home with Duane. Where I was once financially struggling, I was now making more money than I ever had before doing work that I loved and utilizing all my skill sets.

Triple-Aries Duane is a manifestor extraordinaire and loves sharing his abundance with others. He is also an advanced mystical Qigong practitioner trained by a Grand Master from China for twelve years. He is a High Priest, complementing my own vibration as a High Priestess. Now, on the other side of this 2014 master-level initiation, Duane and I began visioning how our powerful love could assist the ascension of humanity and the planet.

The Beginning of the Rest of My Life

This is when the Great Mother presence began coming through me in channeling sessions. When this consciousness first linked to me, I felt a beautiful feminine essence, full of compassion, serenity and wisdom. For a time, every Sunday morning I would livestream a twenty-minute video, channeling her wisdom teachings. Then, after a while, Duane and I began hosting gatherings in our living room where people would lie down and receive a channeled message, energetic treatments and then participate in a prayer for our planet. Suddenly, my ability became clean and clear enough to link to unique vibrations of consciousness, councils of beings within the Great Mother essence. We began calling these many beings the Higher Dimensional Helpers. I remember the first time the Sirian Council of Light came in with a frequency of kindness, care and clarity for our psychological development. (I knew instantly that I had lived in the Sirius system, the vibration was so familiar.) Then the Pleiadian Collective, with their healing technologies and focus on our emotional well-being and the link between our emotions and biology. And eventually an Arcturian consciousness linked with us, and a medical collective supported our genetic and bio-energetic upleveling. Wow!

This was truly a new chapter of my life. Indeed, it was a whole new timeline!

Duane and I began to grow and transform rapidly through working with the Higher Dimensional Helpers. We recorded and transcribed almost every session and the information shared with us was always validated later through a synchronicity, dream, channeling from another lightworker, or information we found through research. The teachings unfolded naturally, in layers of truths. Once we comprehended one layer, they would bring in the next higher-frequency truth, which held all previous truths within it. After a year of intensive work with our guides, we were told by the dolphin consciousness that it was time to move to the Big Island of Hawaii.

All this may seem whimsical and fantastical to you, but you have to understand, for someone who has always perceived reality as multi-dimensional and was always interacting with invisible beings and realms, this wasn't strange at all. In fact, it was the message I'd been waiting for since Duane and I had met. We'd finally been given our Light Leader marching orders!

Once in Hawaii, we were to participate in strengthening a multi-dimensional bridge between higher density Lemuria and our 3D reality. We were shown that eventually we would be keepers of an acreage of land, where we would build The Temple of Remembering (Re-Membering). This Temple would resonate at a frequency recognized by Starseeds and the Souls of Tara, (I will explain who these beings are later in the book), and would play a part in assisting these Souls in remembering who they are.

We moved to the Big Island in January 2018. After arriving the channeling evolved rapidly. Everything about this island is conducive for clear-channeling: the active volcano energies that purify the field, the fact that we're in the middle of the Pacific (peaceful) ocean, far away from another land mass, and the daily presence of the higher consciousness of the whales and dolphins. Never mind that we bought land right within the energy ley line of Kealakekua Bay, a very sacred location. The longitude-latitude of our location on the island has one of the most powerful upwellings of magnetic energy on the planet.

Our house was blessed by a native Hawaiian Aunty whose lineage was of the true wisdom of the Ho'oponopono Keala. During the blessing Aunty and her apprentice sang to Pele, the Aumakua (Guardian Spirits of Place), and the ancestors of the land. We received their blessing and The Temple of Remembering was born! Later this same Aunty would give me my Hawaiian name, and then two weeks later transition into the Spirit World. Our house was the last one she blessed. Since that day, Duane and I have been welcoming Souls from all over the world into ceremony and ritual for deep healing and reclamation of their Divine Human Being blueprint. These are powerful times. Duane and I live each day in gratitude, surrender and faith, as we pro-actively collaborate with Intelligent Infinity to birth a free and harmonic world.

CHAPTER 2

MEETING RA

Right before Duane and I moved to Hawaii, the Law of One: The Ra Material channeled books came into our awareness. We'd heard of the books through David Wilcock, who is one of the current known adepts of interpreting the material. As Duane and I began to get into the first book, we realized that many of the wisdom drops of information were similar, if not verbatim, the information coming from the Higher Dimensional Helpers in our sessions.

My method of channeling, which I call Holistic Channeling, includes affirming a "vertical alignment" between my third density Mind-Body-Spirit and my Over-Soul. Then I link to my own higher dimensional aspects in fourth, fifth, and sixth densities. From there I affirm continuing the vertical alignment to the level of the Buddhas and Angels and then to Yeshua Christ in the eternal realms and then to the Divine Cosmic Mother and Father (Pure Consciousness and Pure Energy); from here, I link to The One, Infinite Creator-Source. All these levels of consciousness exist here and now, all the time, in me and in everyone. Yet, to support my third density brain and nervous system in saying yes to being a channel, I must create a solid container to hold my more untrusting aspects (ego) who don't relish releasing control. I affirm that any being that cannot exist in the harmony of the ascending higher frequencies along this vertical stream is blocked from my field and the Temple's field, and contained where they can do no harm.

For the channeling to be pure, my heart must be open in true love and Oneness. I surrender into sincere gratitude for the wondrous miracle of the infinite, loving families of eternal love-light. My mission has always been, since birth, to help humanity through this major ascension leap, and I joyfully do this through my innate design as a channel.

More Context for the Law of One

The Law of One books were published in 1984, offering the transcriptions of 106 channeled conversations with a sixth density social memory complex, who formed on Venus 2.6 billion years ago, known as Ra. The Law of One books were brought through by three people: Don Elkin, James McCarty and Carla Rueckert. Don was a physics professor and UFO investigator, who led the project with a meticulous scientific focus. He formulated and asked the questions. James McCarty had the job of scribe and sending the channel's body love while they were in session. Carla Rueckert acted as the vessel through which Ra spoke.

Personally, I've never read such pure channeled material before. The closest I've found is the Pathwork material of Eva Pierrakos[4].

As I read The Law of One books, I was struck with feelings of "I know this." To me, the wisdom and information shared felt accurate, though not the whole picture. For the whole picture, I put the Ra Material puzzle piece next to Lisa Rene's Ascension Glossary, Indigenous prophecy from around the world, and my own channeled transmissions. I then began to see a grander story of Who, Where and What We Are.

Terms & Definitions[5]

I will be using certain terminology in this book which comes directly from the Ra Material. I want to explain some of these terms and how Ra defines them here.

----

[4] To learn more about the lectures channeled by Eva Pierrakos, go to: https://pathwork.org/the-lectures/

[5] I want to generally footnote the Terms & Definitions section as I pulled the definitions from the Law of One informational website. This website is an amazing resource! You can search many terms or topics, such as Atlantis or Chakras, and it will pull up all the transcriptions where Ra speaks on that topic. I paraphrased these definitions rather than direct quoting.   https://www.lawofone.info

Mind/Body/Spirit – A life form who does not experience a split or polarized consciousness. The second density life forms of animals are examples of Mind/Body/Spirits.

Mind/Body/Spirit Complex – A life form who has entered into third density, where consciousness is split or polarized. Human beings on Earth right now are Mind/Body/Spirit Complexes. Third density's natural laws and blueprints of life are designed for the perception of duality and so the third density consciousness can move quickly through lessons of a polarizing nature. For example: day and night, wake and sleep, intuition and analysis.

Density – This refers to the literal density a Spirit takes on to experience the lessons to be had from that level of materialization. For example, in third density people experience a dual, or split, consciousness, a certain measure of gravity, and specific natural laws which include predator/prey survival instinct. As compared to fourth density where people experience unity-consciousness, a lighter gravitational field than 3D, and life centers around relationship and service rather than survival and personal legacy.

Ra uses the term density interchangeably with the term octave. Ra explains that there are seven densities within each octave, using the example of keys on a piano: There are seven keys, each different but connected, and the eighth key ends the previous octave while also beginning the next. Within each density are seven sub-densities. Within the sub-densities are seven sub-sub-densities, and so on and so on, infinitely forward and backwards. The Earth and humanity are currently graduating from the third density or octave, and moving into the fourth density or octave. Each density holds seven sub-densities of learning to be integrated, and until this happens a person, or planet, cannot move on to the next octave.

Harvest – Ra calls the moment of shifting from one density to the next higher density at the end of an age "Harvest." This is when the Souls who have acquired a sufficient level of mastery or crystallization of the lessons of the density, "ascend" into the next density of higher frequency. In the books Ra speaks to how many were "Harvestable" at the end of past ages and how the Ra collective's visits to Earth were timed to catalyze a greater Harvest.

Positive and Negative Polarity – Positive polarity is service-to-others and holding the highest good of all as the focal point of one's purpose. Positive polarity is the acknowledgement that we're all One. True Love of others can only come from this awareness.

Positive polarity includes compassion for our shadow-side and eventual opening into personal sacred union of our inner-polarities.

Negative polarity is service-to-self, which is acted out in power plays or manipulation of others for one's own gain. Those in negative polarity are generally in denial of connection to the Infinite Divine Source, and in rebellion against the power of love with no regard for others.

Extreme negative polarity refutes the Laws of Nature, perverts them and manipulates them, creating mutated man-made laws. Extreme negative polarity can be Soulless, perpetuating division and fragmentation of human psyches, because fractured psyches are easier to control.

Intelligent Infinity – The One, All That Is, Source. Intelligent Infinity is pure potentiality and possibility. The first primal paradox of the Law of One, was the distortion of Intelligent Infinity into the dreaming of free-will and therefore an exploration of finity. There are endless possibilities for the expression of the One, and each new aspect of the One who becomes sentient may then begin their own experimentation in creation. This exploration of co-creating with the One, is free to continue into "an eternal present."

Intelligent Energy – The kinetic aspect of Intelligent Infinity used to create new patterns and experiences. All creation has free will, therefore, all creation, once self-aware, can harness Intelligent Infinity and create through Intelligent Energy.

Logos –The Creative Principle or Love. According to Ra, the Logos is the second emanation of Intelligent Infinity. There are many Logoi, or co-Creators experimenting through experiencing, creating Universes, Galaxies, and everything within them. This happens through sourcing Intelligent Infinity through the instrument of being-ness that is the Logos. The Logos then transmits Intelligent Energy into new being-nesses.

Sub-logos – Birthed by the Logoi, the Sub-Logoi or co-co-Creators are refiners of the patterns from Logoi. They are the Suns of solar systems, for example. In a higher dimensional perception of our Sun, one can feel and behold the great awakened consciousness that it is. In my meditations I've sat within the higher dimensional "cities of light" inside our Sun.

Sub-sub-logos - Humanity in our awakened state are creators of reality. We can access Intelligent Infinity, and crystallize it within us, meaning, to bring it into an accessible, complete form of wisdom, knowing, or energy, and then share this through our own mind/body/spirit complex, as conduits or instruments for Intelligent Energy. We are the vehicle through which Intelligent Infinity becomes Intelligent Energy! Though it does take work for us to fine tune ourselves to act as pure instruments, ideally holding the highest good for All in our intentions for creation.

And now, we begin the journey.

CHAPTER 3

THE PURPOSE OF THIRD DENSITY IN HUMANITY'S JOURNEY OF ASCENSION

For so long I have struggled to understand why there is a split within us, why we are born into a veil of forgetting, severed from past-life, between life, and even remembering our night time astral travels. So many people are suffering because of this inner-divide that then creates all the outer-divides as we try to find where we belong. As I was reading Book IV of the Law of One, I came upon a transmission that covered precisely this topic. I was riveted as I read about the origins of the veil that split the third density and the necessity for it. Never before have I perceived my existence and the existence of this world so clearly; and with that clarity, a pure essential jubilation bubbled up from deep within me.

How to Describe the Indescribable?

The One Infinite Creator or Intelligent Infinity are the titles used by Ra for the Source Consciousness. I like these terms. I've used many names for Source and usually refer to this omniscient presence as The One. Everything is the One and derives from the One. From the One came the expression of the One: Intelligent Energy. Intelligent Energy is, you could say, the creative force in the Universe from which everything is given the energy needed to exist.

As The One began to express itself through channeling Intelligent Energy, its creations, through the journey of evolving, awakened into their own Divine Consciousness. The One gave birth, you could say, to these Other-Selves, and these Other-Selves provided diverse experiences that would all be absorbed into the wholeness of The One.

Another way of describing it is: The One differentiated into individualized portions of The One. These co-creators expressed Intelligent Energy as well, creating experiences for consciousness to grow and learn. You can imagine all the differentiated portions of The One fractalling out from the hub of The One. Each emanation of Creator Consciousness is birthed from a vaster Creator Consciousness.

The One is the sum total of all, and from The One came the many, until there are Creator Consciousness's creating in a fractal pattern out from Source all the way to each individual human being. Life, when it moves in fractals, is connected to the Infinite-life original blueprints or the Harmonic Field of The One.

Our Galaxy and Sun as Life-Giving Creators

The Milky Way Galaxy is a Logos presence. Our Sun is a sub-Logos, birthed from the Milky Way Logos. Our Sun expresses the "work" of refining the Intelligent Energy patterns dreamed from our Logos, the Milky Way galaxy, and differentiating them even more.

The center of every galaxy holds the purest expression of the One's will and original blueprints or geometries for all life within that galaxy. The sub-Logos presence then dreams upon those blueprints with their own unique will and inspirations. The further out along the spiraling arms of the galaxy you go, the further the solar systems and celestial bodies are from the pure light of original design. Therefore, solar systems closer to the center of their Galaxy-Logos are existing in higher densities or octaves of learning, and solar systems further out are in the lower densities or octaves of learning.

This center point of our galaxy is a source of regenerative Intelligent Energy. Our Sun was birthed from the Intelligent Energy channeled by and through our galaxy. Indeed, all the solar systems within the Milky Way Galaxy spiraled out from her center.

It is through the diverse expressions of creation that The One comes to know herself. Everything that exists in The One, also exists within every particle of creation existing within The One… which is everything. Every experience and learning that happens within the beings on every level of creation, is absorbed and known by The One instantaneously. That means that not only do we have immediate access to the knowledge of sixth density beings living near the middle of our galaxy, but we also contribute to the awakening of consciousness on other third density planets, with all that we are discovering on our planet about love.

What are the Densities?

Before going more into depth about how this split in consciousness happened in third density, I want to describe briefly the basic attributes of the first three densities. This information is taken from the Law of One books and from information from the Higher Dimensional through my own channeling sessions.

Just a note on the terms "dimension" and "density", which are often confused with each other. The most accurate term for what I'm about to describe is density. Density refers to how dense the Spirit chooses to experience itself and the lessons available to the Spirit at that level of density. While dimensions exist within each density and can have varying purposes, attributes and laws as well. For example, in the 2016 film Dr. Strange by Marvel Studios, there was a "mirror world" that only a few highly trained mystics had access to. We could also acknowledge the realm of the Fae (fairies) and

Plant Spirits as a unique dimension. They share the same density with us, but can only be seen if you enter into their dimension, or if they enter into ours.

Densities are evolutionary schools, you could say, that focus on specific lessons. Within each density, there are eight levels of evolution through which Souls ascend, expanding their awareness of Self. This is much like grade-school. We enter into the educational system at kindergarten and move through to eighth grade. Each year is devoted to a new cycle of learning for that age group. Our Third Density has Souls who are exploring every level or vibration of this octave. Younger Souls within third density may be exploring very polarized, dogmatic experiences, while older Souls may be exploring non-attachment and multi-dimensional awareness as they prepare to ascend.

Scott Mandelker, PhD, another Law of One adept who teaches the material, expresses the infinite nature of the Self's growth through the densities:

> Infinity equals Unity. Unity is the form of Infinity. Infinity cannot be described, but it exists as a unified field. So, Ra says there is no end to yourself, no end to your understanding, no end the journey of seeking, no end to our perceptions of creation. It means that perception never stops. And, the journey never stops...It never ends. Because after the human achieves their moral decision [THE CHOICE] and graduates into fourth density, generally into 4D positive, they go on and learn there. They go on in

fifth, and they go on in sixth and they go on in seventh, and they go on...and they leave the octave...going into eighth density, at the level of a Buddha. At the level of basically an infinite power, they become a force of the infinite creation. And that goes on too! And they still journey and they still are seeking. Whatever that massively expanded sense of being is approaching, basically one who can encompass a seventh dimensional solar system. One who becomes a Sun. S-U-N. And so, becoming a Sun, or a Solar Logos, ...Solar Creator, Creator of a seventh dimensional solar system, is a stage of evolution that is beyond higher self, and beyond Ra...It's the level of a Cosmic Buddha, which basically means Omniscient: knowing everything; Omnipotent: all-powerful, no limit to power, anything that could be done, they can do; and Omnipresent: which means they are present everywhere simultaneously...so that's a vastly expanded state of being! That too is not the end of the journey of seeking! And so, there's no end to our Selves because the Self is the Infinite One. The infinite creation is the Self. There's no true Self outside or separate from the Infinite One of All.[6]

---

[6] Accessed video on September 1, 2021 on YouTube. TWSMandelker channel: The Law of One, Session 1 (2). https://youtu.be/TPGl53eAs14

Beautifully said, Scott! We hold within us all of the densities and have access to explore every dimension, false and harmonic. As everything came from The One, we are never severed from the infinite wisdom and knowledge of The One, even when we choose to focus on just one perception of reality within a specific density.

The Qualities of the First Three Densities?

Let's look at the qualities and lessons of the first three densities, as they relate to sentient, evolving life:

The First Density

The lesson is **Being**. This is the realm of the elementals, meaning the periodic table elements. Minerals, Water, Fire, Wind are expressions arising from the elements in 1D. First density lasts for billions and billions of years, measured by our 3D perception of time.

The Second Density

The lesson is **Growth**. Now, Intelligent Energy, through free will, has reached towards further awakening and expansion of consciousness. The elements begin to coalesce into molecules and organisms. This would be the development of single-cell organisms into bacteria, viruses, plants, and eventually the diversity of all invertabrate and vertebrate animal forms. Ra calls second density consciousness: Mind-Bodies.

The Third Density

The lesson is **Love**, especially in relation to "Other-Selves". Self-reflexive consciousness is born. Whereas in second density Mind-Bodies strive towards self-awareness, in third density they enter into the self-awareness school and become "Mind/Body/Spirit complexes". Within the third density, perception of reality includes space/distance and time.

In third density we realize there is nothing outside of ourselves, and to love another is to love ourselves. To love ourselves is to love all creation.

At this time, each of us holds a history of our evolution through the densities in our bodies. The elements in our body are 1D – water, carbon, minerals, oxygen and other gases. The microorganisms that our body is teaming with are 2D – beneficial bacteria, fungus, yeasts, and parasites, as well as the reptilian brain. As fetuses we have gills on our necks and the remnant of a tailbone. Our 3D evolutionary leap shows in our more complex energy anatomy and the brain's frontal lobe. As we evolved, we didn't forsake all that came before, we built upon it. And when we are truly thriving in life, it's because all these elements, micro-organisms, primitive nervous systems, along with our frontal lobe, are functioning in harmony. When we're healthy, they are communicating with each other seamlessly, so that, when a challenge does present itself, we can adapt, respond, and integrate. Our bodies are truly amazing!

Just an interesting note here: Ra explains that through loving investment of energy from third density beings towards second density beings, we can accelerate the graduation of second density beings into third density. Therefore, the animals who we become close with and whom we share our lives intimately with, are beings who are growing rapidly towards third density self-reflexive consciousness. (For example: Dogs, Cats, Horses.)

Animals exist in the Positive Polarity and are in harmony with the natural and universal laws which govern this realm. Thus, they are able to be way-showers for the human mind/body/spirit complexes. They serve our awakening, and we serve theirs through loving them.

Some higher consciousness creatures, who arrived on Earth from other planets, such as Dolphins and Whales, are also mind/body/spirits, like humans. Some dolphins can get hooked into the reversal energies and express negative polarity, but this is rare. The Cetaceans chose to live in Earth's oceans, I believe, because they are safe from the mind-control of man-made law and manipulation. Also, being in water is supportive of multi-dimensional awareness and healing sound transmissions. (They are healing the ley lines of Earth's grids). And lastly, salt water is very conductive for electrical plasma energy, which is full of "codes" – light codes, ascension codes, and data streams from the eternal realms. The whales translate these data streams and anchor them into our planet, helping to recalibrate this hologram into harmonic patterns.

Thank you dear Cetacea!

Now, let's explore the nature of the veil of forgetting which humanity went through and why.

CHAPTER 4

THE PURPOSE OF DUAL-CONSCIOUSNESS FOR EVOLUTION

As Ra explains it, before the split in consciousness in third density, there was only a unified perception of reality. Third density planets evolving along their natural timeline, took a very long time to enter into fourth density because there were no strong catalysts for the Spirits living upon the planet. Even if material life held demands and stresses, the souls were in a unity consciousness and not severed from any part of their minds or remembering all their lifetimes. They were not blocked from the cosmic energies streaming onto their planet to feed them, so to speak, which meant they were always resourced and thriving physically. If they injured themselves, they simply connected into the field of Intelligent Energy to repair their tissues. There simply was no impetus to move faster. They had an understanding that everything is one, so to have anger or hatred at another didn't make sense. Because the lesson of 3D is about love of other-selves, without the catalyst of duality, evolution moved at a snail's pace.

How We Experience the Split or Veil

Then, The One dreamed a split in consciousness for third density to inspire the life forms to evolve and grow. The veil descended, and humanity now had a split mind: the conscious and unconscious. Now there was the state of being physically awake and going to sleep at night. Also, now there was an inability to perceive spiritual realms with the physical eyes; you could call this a divide between the seen and unseen realms. With these divisions came an adaptation to our brains, with our left hemisphere firmly grounded in linear perception and logic, while the right hemisphere remained connected to a multi-dimensional and non-linear experience of reality.

So, in order to hasten ascension into the fourth density, a split in consciousness was created. 3D is the density where this split is experienced. This split demands that we face choices every day, all the time, to decide what we are and what we are not. This creation ensures we will gain more diverse experience through our free will explorations. The split exponentially accelerated the path to awakening.

The very huge point that I'm making right now is: All that we experience in 3D - all the suffering, conflict, and battling for control within our psyches and minds, as we strive for a sense of security and peace, does not last forever. It's not a hamster wheel of never-ending good guys vs. bad guys fighting for their desired outcomes in our heads, and therefore, in our world. Dual-consciousness and the suffering that goes with it does end. **Even when negative polarity devises perpetual traps for us, duality still ends, because it's the nature of consciousness to expand and illuminate the shadows of delusion.** Just like the seed that sprouts in a crack of the sidewalk can become a tree whose roots destroy the pavement. That which would hold us down will dissolve as our consciousness naturally grows and expands.

I like to think we have ingeniously used the dysfunctional systems and structures of our current reality to further catalyze our awakening and remembering. The split has allowed for seemingly endless opportunities to do "the work" of facing our limitations and making life-changing choices. It was *our* thoughts that created this reality, remember! All that we experience has been willed into being through our personal and collective human consciousness. The more tension, the more catalyst to change.

3D is about making the choice between Love or Fear.

The Power of Collective Consciousness

We now have over eight billion people on planet Earth, so we're told. This is a lot of mind-power that has the potential to synchronize toward a common goal! The more people who come together in prayer or intention-ing for planetary ascension, the faster this goal will be attained. In 1972 Maharishi International University in the United States launched a group meditation experiment in 22 cities. With only 1% of the population of the city using Transcendental Meditation daily, the meditators focused on good will and criminal activity ceasing. The data showed criminal incidences, recorded through the police departments, went down anywhere from 24 to 89% in all of the cities! In control cities, the crime rates went up. Not only that, but the effect lasted six years after the experiment ended. The result is called the "Maharishi Effect." Are you getting how powerful we are? That was just 1% of the population!

Another way of looking at our inevitable awakening is like a swell rolling over the ocean. As it comes into shore, it starts to form a wave. Awakening happens like a wave, growing stronger and more formidable as it reaches its destination. When it crashes, the old paradigm is destroyed. As it ebbs, a new age begins.

Positive and Negative Polarities Create Further Complexity

Ra refers to humanity on Earth as Mind/Body/Spirit Complexes. Before the split in consciousness, when 3D was only in the positive polarity, life on Earth was simply Mind/Body/Spirits. We became complex upon the splitting of consciousness into positive and negative polarities. Now, ascension from third density can lead souls into further exploration along one or the other polarity.

To repeat myself for the sake of clarity:

The third density is to learn about LOVE of "other-selves." To reach ascension in the most accelerated way and so third density doesn't take billions and billions of years, duality was created. Through duality, our consciousness explores service-to-others and service-to-self in order to remember who and what we truly are. Our higher dimensional natures invite us to remember that we are a part of Infinite Intelligence through steering our lives towards catalyzing experiences, such as meeting wise guides, witnessing the beauty of nature, and opening into states of ecstatic love. At the same time our self-serving tendencies can easily steer us away from remembering our true nature. We have Free Will; a gift from our Creator! So, there's nothing to stop our explorations into what we're not. Our negative polarity will try to seduce us with power, money, pleasure, fame, violence, addiction, and other dramas. Souls who are swayed by negative influences don't necessarily like the negative polarity; most are actually using them as catalyst for positive ascension as well. Discovering what we are not, is just as powerful as discovering what we are.

All of this is because the Third Density is about making THE CHOICE.

In Book I of The Law of One, Ra describes something I found very interesting. They said that our planet has spiraled into a fourth density timeline, even though human consciousness has remained in third density. This is creating a large amount of chaotic energy. This leap allowed the Earth to be influenced by the vibrations of 4D, which are **Love and Understanding**, without a full commitment to it within human consciousness. Normally this planetary leap would hasten the "choice-making" of souls and bring about a unification of polarity on the planet, yet, individuals and societies on Earth have remained in confusion, with scattered focus, unable to direct our path clearly towards ascension. Because of this, Ra explains, most souls currently incarnated on the planet will not ascend, but remain within the lower density reality sphere.

My friends, it is the time of Harvest.

Right now.

If we don't make a choice, someone else will make it for us.

Let's continue now and see what happens in fourth and fifth densities.

CHAPTER 5

THE CHOICE

A Brief Description of the Lessons of 4 th and 5th Densities

The lesson of the fourth density is focused on the fullest expression of the Green Ray, which is **Universal Love or Understanding**. In 4D, those who have chosen integral self-love and therefore unconditional love of others, continue to work towards self-realization through collaborative service to others. In 4D, we hone abilities such as telepathy, telekinesis, and bilocation (sending our astral bodies to another part of the world while our physical bodies sit in meditation). For souls who vibrate higher within the octave of fourth density, service may also focus off-planet, supporting those on third density planets to come into unity consciousness.

The lesson of fifth density is focused on attaining the fullest expression of the Blue Ray, which is **Wisdom**. Ra explains, those existing within the fifth density have the responsibility, honor and duty of accepting the Law of One. I take this to mean, they can now self-actualize as a pure emanation of the Law of One, which could also be described as a pure emanation of Unified Consciousness in full "I AM, ALL IS, THE ONE" knowing and being.

The 5D evolutionary leap is into multi-dimensional form, no longer living inside of space/time (linear perception of time), but perceiving reality in and from the NOW. In 5D we still have a physical form, yet we live in time/space where the emphasis is on endless time and the illusion of space is dissolved. Whereas, remember in 3D we perceive endless space, but the concept of time is limited. We rush through life, trying to cover enough ground, knowing we will die one day. This is irrelevant in 5D.

Our consciousness, now centered in non-temporal perception, will allow us to move into other moments of now to assist, as long as we hold a benevolent purpose. Said another way: In 5D there is no point A and point B separated by space; they inhabit the same space. Through directing our intention to where we desire to be, we phase ourselves out of one reality and into another, and we're there.

In the Law of One, Ra explains:

Fifth **density** is perhaps best described as extremely white in vibration.

The **sixth density** of a whiteness which contains a golden quality as you would perceive it; these colors having to do with the blending into wisdom of the compassion learned in fourth **density**, then in **sixth** the blending of wisdom back into a unified understanding of compassion viewed with wisdom. This golden color is not of your spectrum but is what you would call alive.[7]

Resistance to Ascension

Since the invention of the Atom Bomb, our third density Earth has been receiving support from many positive fourth, fifth, and sixth density beings. This invention alerted our more advanced galactic neighbors that we had reached some kind of technological maturity, though clearly not an emotional or spiritual maturity. Guidance was necessary, as any mistakes we made/make with particle fusion and nuclear energy impacts all the other beings in our Universe.

Ra explains that the acceleration of catalysts, namely earth-changes and socio-political upheaval, at this time are chaotic due to the scattered focus humanity has had, unable to unify.

It is our own resistance, fear, and confusion that are creating the climactic upheavals. A teacher once told me, "Resistance often comes up when we are about to take a huge leap towards more happiness in our lives."

---

[7] https://www.lawofone.info/results.php?q=sixth+density+vibratio n. From transcription 33.20. Accessed on June 24, 2021.

Ra states the climactic changes are the result of our fourth density Earth moving into a new position for fourth density magnetic alignment, requiring the vortices of the Earth to shift. This would go smoothly if the mind/body/spirit complexes upon the planet were able to sync-up, or entrain with our planet's resonance field, or to say it another way, if we were in harmony with our Universe. Unfortunately, many people have been so entrenched in the false timelines, which serve to sever us from our Soul light, nature and the Divine, when the earth-changes happen, or when the social and political upheavals occur, they will view them as terrifying. Those who are *not* walking their ascension path into 4D or higher could experience the planetary vibrational shifts as frightening and threatening, misunderstanding the larger picture of what's unfolding. What I see is that, as humanity breaks free of the false timelines, these structures of limitation will collapse, on all levels.

I believe that many higher density unified civilizations have been watching and waiting for our planet to be ready to join the Galactic family. The higher dimensional guardians of our solar system know that Earth's people are near the threshold of ascension, and they have witnessed the insertion of the false timelines and mind-control programs to keep us from ascension. While these guardians have honored our free-will choice to experience these extremes of enslavement, they do intervene in the ways they can to help us wake up.

Each of us, once we become aware of the Ascension Timeline, have the honor, duty and responsibility to assist humanity in waking up. How does one fulfill this devotional duty? Be Love.

Yes. It's that simple. Be Love.

Even if you want to regress into the small "me", grasping for personal gratifications... Rise above and remember the current situation. Remember your consciousness impacts this Ascension Timeline – And choose to Be Love!

I'll offer this story for encouragement:

When I was attending graduate school in San Francisco, on some days I would take the ferry across the bay from my home in Marin County. Once in the city, to get to my final destination, I would hop onto the street car at the ferry building, which would take me down Market street to Fulton street. From there I'd walk about four blocks the front doors of my university.

I've never felt comfortable in big cities. The sheer number of people has always felt overwhelming to my psychic sensitivities and the homeless situation broke my heart, but also made me hyper-vigilant for my safety. As the years passed at graduate school, I became more and more comfortable in the SoMa, South of Market, neighborhood of the city and navigating public transportation wasn't so ungrounding for me anymore. I attribute this shift to a couple things:

1. I was studying psychotherapy and was acquiring deeper and deeper understanding of the nature of the human psyche. I began seeing people as interesting and unique matrices of experience, rather than scary unknown personalities.

2. I was studying my own psyche constantly and I was choosing again and again to stay awake, present and purposeful in my thoughts and behaviors.

One day, after class, I walked to the bus stop to catch the 2:00PM ferry back to Larkspur. I caught a bus that would take me all the way to the ferry building on Market Street. I took a seat at the front right side. A man boarded the bus at the next stop who was clearly schizophrenic. This was a MUNI bus and the seats at the front were facing inward towards a center aisle, so this man was sitting to my right, just one seat away. The man was talking loudly to himself about a football team. The people nearest to him, one by one, stood up and moved further back in the bus. I noticed I didn't feel uncomfortable. I felt an amazing sense of peace.

All my learning about schizophrenia from my psychopathology class flooded into my awareness. My professor had illuminated us about how a schizophrenic mind has zero sense of boundaries. Whereas, I had the opportunity to create a strong ego structure and could define what was me and what wasn't, a schizophrenic person did not have this safety. They were permeable to everything. Even other dimensions and things invisible to us, like ghosts.

I closed my eyes with intent to expand my peace. I could hear the man yelling and I heard another person get up and move seats to escape the discomfort. In my meditation, I spoke to the spirit of the man. I told him, "You are safe. I know you may not feel safe all the time, but I assure you, that right now, you are safe. Find peace." I then realized it was quiet on the bus. I opened my eyes and looked to my right. The man was staring at me with a calm face. I just looked back at him with a slight, peaceful smile. Then I lowered my gaze to my hands in my lap. The bus stopped to let people off. We were halfway to the ferry building. The man stood quietly and disembarked the bus quietly.

I tell this story a lot to my clients and students, because it was such a profound moment for me. When I could release my own egoic grasping and rejecting, and just Be Love, I knew exactly what to do. I knew how to feel ultimately safe in the moment, and also how to be of service to others, especially to this man.

Love is powerful. Love moves mountains. Love is the most powerful healing force on Earth. And Love is who we are. When you love yourself, you can finally see, know and love others without judgement, scrutiny, comparing yourself or competing, and without fear or feeling irrationally threatened. I will repeat this in many different ways throughout this book. Be Love. This is the lesson we're crystallizing here at our graduation from Third Density.

CHAPTER 6

WOMEN WILL LEAD THE WAY

Tying-In the Mayan Prophesies

In April 2017, before Duane and I moved to Hawai'i, I was suddenly reunited with my father after an eight-year estrangement. He was dying. His wife had contacted my brother and I to let us know. This opened the door to a much-needed period of healing and forgiveness. While in this phase, which sadly ended with being disowned again right before his death, I had one of the most magical experiences of my life. While on the phone with a healer to receive support for my grief around my father's state, I walked outside to feel the sun. I immediately knew I had to continue my session lying inside the Medicine Wheel in the meadow.

We were on an acre of land in east Santa Rosa, California, and the grass was bright green with Spring energy. The Medicine Wheel was twenty feet diameter, made from stones collected from the nearby creek, along with larger stones whom we called "elders", placed at the cardinal directions. These stones had traveled to every wilderness rites of passage or "vision fast" I'd ever led and were always part of our community Medicine Wheels. These stones were powerful!

Anyway, I was lying in the Medicine Wheel receiving counseling for my heartbreak, when in the sky above me I saw four dark spots and a larger dark spot, and I heard the twittering call that could only be from a Golden Eagle! I focused my vision and saw that I was staring at a mother Golden Eagle with four eaglets circling high in the sky just north of my location. As I watched, the mother eagle flew towards me, then veered west and made a counter-clockwise circle around to the south, where she entered the light of the noonday sun, then out the other side to the east and back to the north. She did this once more, then joined her eaglets and they soared off over the hills in the north.

I started laughing and crying at the same time, telling the healer, "Oh my God! My father is leaving this earth... I see him with a line of male ancestors behind him. They're handing me the staff of power! They acknowledge me as a leader worthy of guiding my people..." My tears were hot as they rolled down my cheeks where I lay on my back in the western quadrant of the wheel. "Is this really happening??" I blurted out. My healer friend soothingly invited me to breath and not talk for a while; to feel what was happening, rather than try to wrap my head around it. My heart released multiple generations of trauma in that moment.

I tell this story to preface the next one which takes place five years before. You'll understand why as you read on...

In December 2012, I was in the archeological ruins of the ancient Mayan city of Tikal, in Guatemala. I was there to attend a Winter Solstice ceremony with Mayan people and pilgrims from many countries around the world. The experience was life-changing for me. I had the honor to witness an event of power that most people on Earth will never witness. My small group, who I was traveling with, stayed at a hotel within the national park just a short walk away from the central plaza. The night before the ritual opened to the public, December 20, I was suddenly gripped with a fever, diarrhea and vomiting. After all the work it took for me to get there, you can imagine my disappointment! I told myself, I will wake up at 4:00AM anyway, as if I am going to join my group for the trek by head-lamp up to the central plaza of the main compound.

At 4:00AM, the alarm clock went off. My friends woke and began dressing and loading their small day-packs with essentials for the day - camera, snacks, water, layers of clothes. I sat up in bed and assessed my situation. To my huge surprise, all my symptoms were gone! I dressed quickly and exited the hotel with my group. It was an otherworldly feeling, hiking in a procession up a foot trail to the central plaza, with jaguar calls reaching our ears from the dark jungle! Once at the plaza we climbed halfway up the pyramid called Templo II in the west, which faced Templo of the Gran Jaguar in the East, which was lit up by spotlights. As we got settled, we gazed down at the plaza where CNN and local news teams were covering the choreographed entertainment. This "entertainment" portion concluded at around 5:00AM. The audience who came just for that part, slowly rose and filed out of the plaza, including the president of Costa Rica and the president of Guatemala. We laughed as a cheer rose from the mostly traditional Mayan crowd when the Guatemalan president walked out. A cheer that he would no longer be with us, not one of appreciation.

Now, the sun was about to rise over the jungle. This was the moment we'd been waiting for. The new sun rising upon the new Earth. In Mayan prophecy, this was the seminal moment marking the close of one age of 144,000 years, and the beginning of the next; Bak'tun 12 to Bak'tun 13. The elders present were chanting their lineages and invoking the powers within nature to support their interpretation of the new prophecy. And then it happened! Tears rolled down my cheeks as I watched the sun crest the peak of the Temple of the Jaguar. I climbed down to the plaza and made my prayers at the ceremonial fire, which had been burning for days. I looked to the old ones, singing and focused on the fire and I suddenly had a profound sense of the potency of that moment. I dropped into a timeless state and released my prayer for the planet.

At 10:00AM, I began to feel fatigue taking me over and my symptoms returning. I became dizzy, congested and nauseous. I quickly got myself back to my hotel room and into bed, just in time to fall into a deep trance state. Ancestor spirits stood around the bed tending to me. I could hear them. I could smell them. I felt blanketed in love. My roommate told me later that when she opened the door to our room to bring me food, she hit a wall of energy and immediately turned and left.

A few days later, just before Christmas, our group sat in council in a village on the shores of Lake Atitlán with a family of local, respected Mayan Day Keepers, discussing our December 21 experiences. Tata S. had been leading a ceremony in Bolivia on Lake Titicaca. His wife had been in ceremony with the women and children at their compound in Sololá. Tata S. insisted that the women share our stories first, as they are most relevant to the new Bak'tun. I shared my story of my illness and my experience of oneness at the fire. Tata S. looked at me and said, "This was a purification. The Ancestors were purifying and preparing you. This is a big deal. You are a bridge person, like myself."

When Tata S. shared, he summarized his experience in this way, "**The staff of power has been handed from men to women.** We've seen what men have done with power. Now let's see where the women will take us. Women will come into power on all levels – starting with the family, on up to the highest levels of government."

His vision correlated with the Mayan Dresden Codex, which states that at the end of the grand cycle, the Earth will face fear of destruction. An asteroid will be heading towards Earth and our military and scientists will not be able to change its trajectory. In the end, it is the coming together of human consciousness that changes the trajectory of the asteroid so it doesn't hit the planet. This catalyzes a great awakening in humanity, because now people know how powerful they truly are. This begins the dismantling and collapse of all toxic systems upon the planet, including government, military industrial complex, banking, education, agricultural, health and medical, and even toxicity within the social structures.

Tata S. told us to take this message back home and share it widely, which I did and continue to do. I share this story with you now, in 2022, because of the massive planetary shift we find ourselves in today. I believe that the time Tata S. was speaking about is in full swing NOW.

My father died in July, 2020, of alcoholism. My father, for me, was the archetype of the old paradigm which is now collapsing. Though he was a complex mixture of good and evil, in the end I witnessed him choose fear over love, and hatred over healing. He suffered greatly in his life and especially his final years. He is my very clear example of the repercussions people will experience by choosing service-to-self and negative polarity. At the same time, I am blown away that only in this collapse, is there a handing over of the "staff of power" to the positive polarity. The Maya referred to the women as the receivers of the staff, yet I see it also as the return of the feminine/Mother energies within all people and as the positive polarity within us, receiving this staff. A staff of sovereignty and freedom, which we now are strong and awake enough to wield, to create a new, beautiful world.

What does this mean for you and me right now?

Currently we are in the "asteroid" stage of the prophesy, where we either wake up to how powerful our unified consciousness is or we face loss of our power like we can't even imagine. 2020-2021 was the stage of becoming aware there was an asteroid (read as Negative Polarity Controllers and their "Pandemic"). We were seeing the asteroid careening through space towards our planet gripped with fear. This asteroid is the loss of all rights; our freedom; our sacred genetics… At the point of this writing it is January 2022, and we are at the critical moment of breaking free from our brainwashing or perishing. EVERYTHING HINGES ON OUR WAKING UP BECAUSE OUR UNIFIED CONSCIOUSNESS CHANGES EVERYTHING.

I liken it to having lived one's whole life in a snow globe that has been inverted, forced upside down, for so long, those living within it have learned how to adapt ourselves to an upside-down world. Now, forces beyond our comprehension are preparing us for Harvest through major upheaval and catalyst, and the snow globe, our reality, has been turned ride-side up! This inevitably creates a sense of chaos, as everything is shaken up. What was up is now down. What was right is now left. We find ourselves facing The Choice! If we relax and trust, we will right ourselves and align with the harmonics of the free Universe. If we resist and reject this transformation, we will struggle and suffer greatly.

CHAPTER 7

NEGATIVE POLARITY AND ASCENSION

Because of the veil that allowed for forgetting and thus a greater catalyst to wake us up, the journey through 3D became much faster. And in order to gain as much understanding of one's consciousness in this realm as possible, souls began choosing to have shorter and shorter life spans. We went from living 700 to 900 years (Old Testament), to an average lifespan of 70 or 90 years. Souls could now cycle through lifetimes quickly and experience every possible form of death, disease, struggle, sexuality, career, childhood, education, oppression, power, and demographic that they believed would serve their evolution towards fourth density harvest. Exploring service-to-self may not be the final choice when Harvest time comes even if, for example, a Soul has expressed many lifetimes as a perpetrator.

Evolution into fourth density negative polarity, service-to-self, does not happen on a grand scale. It requires a soul to be 95% service-to-self oriented, which is a large forsaking of natural heart chakra activity. This means that these persons choose to skip the Universal Love development, further developing the qualities of the lower chakras – i.e., magic, creativity, power, and reaching personal full-potential.

Those who do acquire that 95% negative polarity ascend at Harvest into a fourth density service-to-self reality. These beings may continue with this exploration of separation from love and The One up until they reach the Harvest at the close of fifth density, moving into sixth density. I will discuss this more later.

The way I understand fourth and fifth density Negative Polarity is by comparing it to the "bad guy" characters in Lord of the Rings. Wormtongue, the character who was manipulating Theoden, the King of Rohan, is the third density example of service-to-self. He did the bidding of Saruman. Saruman was a white wizard who had mastered alchemy and magic and turned to grandiosity and hunger for more power, thus sacrificing his heart. He was a fourth density service-to-self master, creating an army for his fifth density master. Sauron was the fifth density, highest-ranking negative master. He was a disembodied, multiple dimensional consciousness reliant on his minions who did have bodies, to do his bidding. Notice how the negative polarity exists within a pecking order and hierarchy, where they maintain control of those below them through manipulation and fear. Sound familiar? This is the paradigm we are leaving behind.

CHAPTER 8

ALLIES AND GUARDIANS OF EARTH IN OUR MIDST

The Allies and Guardians of Earth come in many forms. They can be off-world, extraterrestrial races as well as ascended masters or higher dimensional or higher density collectives. They can also be right here with us on Earth, living as one of us! Ra calls these people Wanderers.

In whatever form these allies come in, they are with us because they care deeply for our planet, our rightful timeline, and our freedom from oppression. Until 2020, I had no idea of the war going on behind the scenes between good and evil, on and off planet. I had no idea that a real-life Star Wars scenario was happening in and around our solar system. Benevolent E.T.s have been out there fighting for us and our right to know our true heritage and history! And over the centuries they have made contact with many pure hearted individuals, who would carry their messages of peace into the public sphere, facing ridicule and character assassination. Today, contactees, experiencers, and Wanderers are finally being acknowledged, simply because everything they've been divulging over the decades has all come true.

Here is a poignant message from the Arcturian representatives of the Council of Fifty, given to us on October 1, 2019, to prepare us for unprecedented upheavals about to take place. The Council of Fifty is a Galactic Diplomatic Council with representatives from fifty planetary systems who are from the positive 4th and 5th densities.

THE GREAT SHIFT

October 1, 2019

We greet you on the eve of rapid transformation and the beginning of a new chapter of change. We are the Arcturian Council members of the Council of Fifty.

Your planet has reached the brink of new life and old life. You stand at the threshold where the sun is setting into an orange-pink horizon. Say goodbye to who you were, for things are about to drastically change. We would prepare you for certain, we would say, upheavals, disasters, destructions that are coming.

Yes, indeed, these will be on your planet's surface. A great upheaval of the mother's skin. Earthquakes and tsunamis. This is part of the shifting. Please do not fret. Those souls who have chosen to depart at these exit points, it has been pre-arranged. There is nothing to fear. The Great Mother yawns and stretches, her awakening tantalizing goose bumps on her skin. She is exhilarated.

There is a mountain grid that is ready to be synthesized by the Council of the Sun, do you understand? These are mountains around the world. This will help the cohesion of the planet during the shift that is coming. The events will be humbling for those in power. Many will be at a loss. It will be up to local citizens to care for each other.

The Universal Mother Ray is anchoring into the heart of the planet at this time. This Universal Mother Ray is from the eternal realms; vibrant and strong, her resonance spirals in radial geometries, nesting in the amethyst grid around the core, amplified by the crystalline matrix around the core.

The upheavals spoken of earlier come because of this. Do you see? The mother is waking up.

DUANE: Could you tell us more about the mountain top grid? I feel like this grid is really important?

ARCTURIAN COUNCIL: The Mountain Grid resonates at the Indigo Ray. It is the symbolic third eye. The indigo ray/light connects all the mountain peaks of the world. This is the awakened father consciousness that must be in a cohesive holding of the core of the earth as the aqua Arc of the Mother enters, anchors in, and awakens the feminine once again on your planet. The pulsations through the planet's many layers will create strong sonic repercussions that will reach the surface of the earth, triggering earthquakes and volcanic eruptions.

The Father Mountain Grid - Awakened Third Eye Grid will help to spread the sonic waves evenly and disperse them out beyond the biosphere. Very much like the kundalini rising from the base of the spine, which must go out the crown, rather than build without an outlet. The mountain peaks are the outlet, helping to channel this great energy of new life, vibrancy, and presence.

This is what we have all come for - the guardians of Earth - to assist and celebrate this moment. There will be a pulsing of energy moving into the earth as well, from the cosmos. Waves of solar energy from your sun. The sun's energies will be pulsing into the earth, as she pulses from the core out to the surface. The Earth and Sun are connected and this will create a dual flow. There is the electro-magnetic going in and the sonic going out.

Religious dogmatic structures will fall soon, and this is what will instigate the great shift in human consciousness. There will be a great disillusionment rippling through the collective field. Most will bounce back even stronger than before with great revelation, clarity, and joy to be liberated into the truth.

We would warn you, there will be many suicides during this time. Many suicides and many "suicides" – deaths staged as suicides. We do not say this to scare you, but to prepare you psychologically. (pause)

Be as the children in your trust: lightness, innocence, and love. This will keep you strong, resilient, and full. There is nothing you will want for. Your needs will be met. Keep your hearts pure and direct, and your intentions in alignment with the highest vibration of truth.

For this timeline is sanctified. A new day is dawning. Prepare yourselves. Let your hearts be full of rainbows. Give thanks every day. Release all the smallness of the mind. The great shift is upon you.

We bless you with fortitude.

(End of Transmission)

As this is the first transcription from one of my channelings in the book, and it's a very important one as it forewarns what is coming in 2020, I would like to take the time to break it down and highlight some of the main points.

1. This transmission came through on October 2019. The HDH's are arriving with a message of "you are on the eve of rapid transformation." And then, "say goodbye to who you were for things are about to drastically change". At the time of this transmission the virus that would become famous was entering on the scene in China. The United States would not close our borders for another four months. Drastic change – YES! At no time in history has the whole planet locked-down -Economies halted, schools closed, people told to stay at home.

   Duane and I were in California in March 2020, on our way to Amsterdam and then Italy. As the European countries started closing their borders one by one, we had to keep rerouting our trip. The HDH's told us to go to Sweden. They were adamant that we were not to go to Norway or Denmark, just Sweden. In the end, we ended up cancelling everything and at the last minute before Hawaii closed down, we jumped on a plane back to Kona. (Interesting that Sweden was the one Scandinavian country that did not lock-down, did not shut down its economy and did not freak out about the virus.)

2. The HDH's mention natural upheavals and destruction would be happening, yet no inference of a virus. Later when we asked about this, they told

us this was because a global pandemic was not in "my library" of awareness, therefore, they couldn't divulge the details or it would have robbed me of a unique and powerful growth opportunity. It was evidently important that Duane and I experience the pandemic narrative at the same time as the rest of humanity.

Simultaneously we did also have natural cataclysms as well – horrific fires on the west coast of the United States, flooding, tornadoes. We also saw extreme weather conditions over 2020 and 2021, due to weather warfare and the removal of deep underground military bases (DUMBs) through explosives, creating nonstop earthquakes on land and under the sea. (DUMB removal intel source: Gene Decode)[8]

3. The next drop of information was about the Mother Ray or frequency coming into Earth, and the planetary mountain grid supporting the integration of this consciousness. For those paying attention, we can see that the dysfunction of modern day civilization is due almost totally to the submission and suppression of feminine wisdom and power. Therefore, the knowledge that balance will return

---

[8] Gene Decode served in the United States Navy Submarine Force for over 20 years. Information sourced from Gene Decode's interviews on Rumble and other platforms. Website: www.GeneDecode.org

when the feminine energies arise again is a no brainer. Many lightworkers have been tracking the return of the Great Mother for decades and working towards these ends. So, the HDH's are saying, 'The Time Is Now – She's Back!' They tell us this frequency is going to enter into the amethyst grid around the core of the planet where it will amplify, then radiate back up to the surface.

4. The Father Mountain grid is activated, they say, to support in the dissemination of the Mother frequency. There is a powerful field generated innately by the sacred geometry of pyramidal shaped structures. The ancient pyramids built by our ancestors were endowed often with peaks of crystalline or gold, which would attract and capture plasma energies in the atmosphere and direct this energy down into chambers where it could be stored and shared to the surrounding areas. Mountains are larger than these pyramids, naturally formed, yet also capture and share these cosmic energies with the planet and inner-Earth layers, including underground oceans and river systems. This charged water then revitalizes the waters of the planet as it circulates, which then transfers into the roots of trees, etc.

5. They then share that dogmatic, religious structures will be taken out. During the last two years, those who are paying attention have seen the fall of the Vatican and the Pope, the Dalai Lama, and other major spiritual leaders, who have been revealed to

be pawns of the inverted hologram, and of the negative polarity. The invitation has been for people to take their power back from authority figures and re-invigorate a personal connection with God. (If the information here is triggering for you, please trust your heart to either do your own research, or let it go).

6. Finally, they warn that there will be many suicides and murders made to look like suicides. I suppose, if we did our own research on this, we would see the truth in their statement. I imagine they speak to this to emphasize the impact the coming events will have on the human psyche, as the taking of one's own life usually happens when one is in extreme despair, feels powerless and trapped, or feels extreme guilt. I have personally been aware of many murders framed as suicides of whistleblowers who have come out with proof of deception and downright evil from corporate giants, especially in big pharma.

We can feel in this transmission that the Higher Dimensional Helpers are wanting to support our ability to contextualize impending events within the greater journey of ascension. Even with their warning message, we could have never imagined what was about to unfold.

The Wanderers

Who are the Wanderers? We are beings who incarnated into the third density, yet are not from third density. Some souls who are incarnated on Earth have already ascended through third, fourth and even fifth densities. There are many reasons why a higher density being might want to incarnate into 3D. For example, they may have remnants of lessons they're still learning from the third dimension. Yet, when Wanderers choose to come into third density during the end of a grand cycle of evolution of 75,000 years, it is often with the mission to help catalyze the planet's ascension towards the positive fourth density. Wanderers do this through their lightwork of teaching and being living examples of kindness, compassion, wisdom, and peace. Usually, if you are a Wanderer, you secretly know this about yourself. And usually, Wanderers tend to be drawn to other Wanderers to do lightwork together for greater influential impact.

Right now, we are at the close of a grand cycle of evolution for our planet. Time is of the essence. All the Wanderers are activated or activating as lightbearers, way-showers, and bridge-people.

Ra expressed that there were around 65 million Wanderers on the planet at the time when the books were written. I believe there are now more, as two more generations have been born. Ra explains that often Wanderers struggle in third density with the contrast from their own density. As well, when they incarnate into a previous density, they are prone to the laws of that density, therefore, the veil of 3D does impact them, and some of them get hooked into the karmic cycle of reincarnation. Wanderers may also be born with defects, weak physical constitution, psychological imbalances, or a strong sense of alienation.

Joyfully, more and more people are remembering that they are Wanderers – AKA: Souls from higher densities who have returned in service.

That is key!

Until we wake up to this remembering, we will continue getting lost in identity politics, ego attachments and lower-vibrational pursuits, thus continuing on in the reincarnation cycles of 3D, unable to experience and thus express our true divine nature.

The Guardians Respond to Earth's Call for Help

Since 2018 when Duane and I moved to Hawai'i and began regular channeling sessions, the Higher Density Helpers have been telling us that they "felt" the shift happen in and on our planet. Every planet gives off a unique frequency that resonates at the combination of planetary consciousness, with the collective consciousness of the beings living in, and on, the planet. When a planet nears

Harvest, there is a change in the resonance. This could be from the Heart Field of humanity shifting into more openness, or could also be from human consciousness vibrating at a higher rate, as more people have been seeking out the truth and dedicating themselves to freedom from illusion.

One way we can track the Earth's vibrational shift is to follow the fluctuations of the Schumann Resonance. This is a measurement of the Earth's Ionisphere, where plasma waves get caught from lightening and solar flares. Since the Schumann Resonance has been monitored, it has shown an average "humming" of about 7.83 Hz. Ancient Indian Rishis call this the frequency of the Universe, of OM. Other's refer to it as Earth's Frequency, which all life on the planet must be connected with to thrive. I have notice that since 2012, the Schumann Resonance has been reaching peaks way, way higher than 7.83 Hz! And the average frequency of Earth is getting stronger. In May of 2021 we had a spike in the Schumann Resonance to 12.21 Hz.

During the April 4, 2020 (4.4.4) Global Meditation, over millions of people all over the world were visioning the Earth's ascension (peace, harmony, and thriving for all life) and the Schumann Resonance peaked at 156 Hz for days, on and after the meditation. The peak was recorded by a Russian Space Observing System website that records Schumann's resonance.

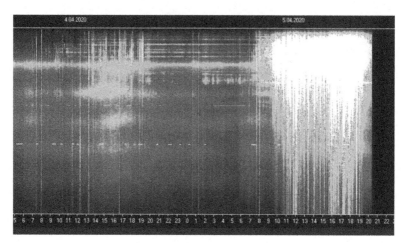

Schumann resonances on April 4, 2020

Another example of how powerful we are!

Here is another relevant excerpt I found from clinical psychologist Dr. Kathy Forti[9]:

> *Scientist's report that the Earth's magnetic field, which can affect the Schumann Resonance, has been slowly weakening for the past 2,000 years and even more so in the last few years. No one really knows why. I was told by a wise old sage from India that the magnetic field of Earth was put in place by the Ancient Ones to block our primordial memories of our true heritage. [Perhaps this is the veil which Ra*

---

[9] Accessed from the website on April 27, 2020:
https://trinfinity8.com/why-is-earths-schumann-resonance-accelerating/

describes.] This was so that souls could learn from the experience of free-will unhampered by memories of the past. He claimed that the magnetic field changes are now loosening those memory blocks and we are raising our consciousness to greater truth. The veil is lifting.

Scientists call the phenomenon of the Earth's magnetic field weakening the South Atlantic Anomaly.[10] I looked for more information on this and found an article on Scientalert.com. "The South Atlantic Anomaly is a vast expanse of reduced magnetic intensity in Earth's magnetic field, extending all the way from South America to southwest Africa... our planet's magnetic field acts as a kind of shield – protecting Earth from solar winds and cosmic radiation..."

What could be happening here? Could it be part of Ascension that the magnetic field "loosens" so the blocks to our memories are removed? Are the higher measurements of the Schumann Resonance connected to the weakening magnetic field around our planet? Is our growing mass consciousness participating in this shift? What about the Photon Belt? Could the influx of high concentrations of

---

[10] https://www.sciencealert.com/mysterious-anomaly-weakening-earth-s-magnetic-field-seems-to-be-splitting-into-two Accessed on December 10, 2021

photons (cosmic rays) be revealing many hidden mysteries about our reality? (More on the photon belt later.)

One thing I feel I can say for certain, there are many layered events happening right now in the seen and unseen worlds…in the conscious and unconscious…in Heaven and on Earth. The veil is lifting as we are now in 4D Harvest. We will be seeing a lot more "anomalies" as the New Earth births, I'm sure!

The Guardians of Earth have felt this shift, like a signal reaching them across dimensions, and they have come to support our leap. Yet, the work of Ascension is ultimately ours to do. The Helpers are supporting us, yet not interfering with our free will, as we go through this global transformation. It is for us to show up and help each other through the fear and confusion that will get triggered. There will be inner and outer upheavals during this transformation. Ra expresses this in the books, the Higher Dimensional Helpers are very clear about this in my channeling sessions, and we are all living through it now. Are we prepared as Lightworkers to serve during this potent transitioning from one density to the next higher octave?

CHAPTER 9

THE CREATION OF FALSE TIMELINES

Information has been coming through from many sources, including Galactic Council contact with humanity and insider-whistleblowers who have had access to the vast libraries in the Vatican archives, that all we've been told about who we are and where we came from, is false. To summarize, we have been lied to systematically for thousands of years for one purpose: To block our ascension.

Living in the Inverted Hologram

I believe that a *natural* 3D evolution does NOT include such perverse inversions of truth. The inversions, or reversals, are inserted from a group of beings, called by Ra, the "Orion Group" and Lisa Renee calls them or it, the "Negative Alien Agenda" or "NAA". Some refer to them as the Khazarian Mafia, the Freemasons, the Illuminati or simply the Cabal. The people who are controlled by these negative beings, knowingly or not, then create man-made rules and laws and use trickery to push this agenda of ultimate planetary control.

The trickster consciousness within humanity takes on the guise of trustworthiness while also attaining positions of authority within the organizing bodies of our society, such as government, healthcare, finances, education, military, sports and entertainment. Media is used as its propaganda machine. Now the trickster consciousness can slowly, over time, manipulate the global masses towards its end goal with little resistance. Once this negative polarity consciousness gains the trust of the people, then it can promote ideas as fact, and the people will create new cultural norms based on these falsehoods. After many generations, the falsehoods become ingrained within the psyche of society as foundational truths. Of course, there are always opposing sub-cultures that arise who hold keys to the actual truth and these "Lightworkers" or wisdom keepers dedicate their lives to illuminating the truth to the masses.

The teacher Jesus Christ, A.K.A. Yeshua, is a prime example of this. The Law of One refers to Yeshua as an emanation of the Galactic Mind. Lisa Renee refers to the center of the Milky Way as being the consciousness of the Divine Mother. Put these two stories together, and it makes sense that Mother Mary was an emanation of the Galactic Heart, and she birthed the Galactic Mind, who came to Earth. He was a fourth-density being at the highest level of that density's learning, which is **Universal Love**. He chose to incarnate on our planet to channel through his instrument the potency and power of Love – to heal, to unify, to free, to create, to inspire. "These things you shall do and more." he told his disciples, full well knowing that all people would move through an ascension into fourth density when the time came.

During his time embodied, he defied the money-mongering of the Pharisees, the cultural acceptance of exiling the mentally ill and lepers, and the manipulation of people to turn against each other. He taught that we are all One and we are here to love one another. Because he was going against the power-over paradigm and undermining the rule of Rome and the Pharisees, AND questioning the inversions that had been accepted and ingrained into culture, he was put to death.

Here is a list of inversions and reversals which I perceive have been, or currently are being, ingrained and normalized in our modern global culture:

- Growth of civilizations through dominion, conquering, and competition is a normal way to progress. Government leaders repeating over and over again that we are in the age of endless wars.

- The medical establishment and Big Pharma make people sick then offer a drug as the solution, while they make billions from people's suffering. Those who discover natural cures for diseases at a low cost are killed, their houses raided, patents stolen, and cures are destroyed and hidden.

- Usury or the creation of debt and use of taxes and interest to financially enslave people.

- The domination of polluting energy sources such as nuclear, petroleum and coal vs. free energy devices and natural energies

- The act of sex becomes exploitive, violent and addictive, rather than a sacred unifying ritual to elicit connection to our divine multi-dimensional consciousness.

- Predating on the most innocent and defenseless, the children, for self-centered gains. Child sex-trafficking is the top-grossing trade on Earth right now. One child can make a "handler" $65K per customer.

- Devaluing, exiling and killing our most precious teachers, our Elders. During 2020, over 26,000 elders in nursing homes were given overdoses of Midazolam and Morphine, which euthanized them without being told. Cause of death was marked down as COVID-19.[11]

- Women are emotionally controlled through fear of physical harm and psychologically shamed or negatively labeled for being sexual, with constant enforcement of these beliefs in TV, movies, historical accounts, and religious dictates. The Fierce Mother and the Empowered Creative

---

[11] Video link: https://www.bitchute.com/video/klZLS4ncMp2n/. Accessed on November 27, 2021.

Priestess have been locked-down and kept away from their power to bring harmony to the false timelines. Feminine leadership comes naturally from a woman's innate sense of interconnection and desire for health within her family. When kept in fight-flight-freeze trauma reactions, women sink into depression and despair, steeped in survival anxiety, self-loathing or low self-worth.

• Men are emotionally controlled through shaming around showing care or questioning the authorities over them, and thus, their true power to protect and lead are locked down. Fathers abandon their children, too numb and full of rage to understand what they're abandoning. Masculine leadership is in balance when coming from the Heart. Without guidance of the Heart, people are sociopathic.

• Commodification of EVERYTHING, which makes the meaning of life about consumption and gears the human psyche towards service-to-self. This means that every living thing is subject to scrutiny around its value, right to exist, and expendability; which puts every life into a core fear of being found worthless.

• The propaganda machines of the global elite, such as mainstream media, promote war, fear, anxiety, division, racism, sexism, hatred, and envy. They want to perpetuate insecurity and keep people distracted from striving for God and our true natures.

- Air, water, soil, agriculture, livestock, medicines, lightbulbs, our phones and computers, and beauty products, are all purposefully designed to lower our immunity and life force energy. They are weaponized with poisons to cause disease, sterilization, and thus, dependence on government institution hand-outs. How is it that we live on a planet where the very air, water, and soil has been made toxic to life, yet those who continue to spread the poison deny it is poison, or they defend their actions based on financial need?

So, you get the picture! We have been living in a societal system designed to enslave and poison people. Human consciousness has been constantly infiltrated by negative polarity values of ruling over others for one's own gain, and the promotion of fear, suffering and pain to accomplish this. They want to feed on us, or turn us into their minions.

The good news is...there are more of us than there are of them. A LOT more! And our love is more powerful than their hate. None of their schemes have worked to block or end the Ascension Timeline. We are waking up. We are remembering who we are. We are Ascending.

Yeshua told us that he would return at the end of the age to guide us into the Kingdom of Heaven. Christians refer to this time as the End of Days and the Second Coming of

Christ. In the Law of One, Ra speaks to this. They explain that when Jesus said this, he was speaking from his identity as a higher-fourth density ascended master. He knew he wasn't an individual, but part of a powerful, loving collective consciousness. Jesus was telling us that at the time of Harvest, at the close of the Grand Cycle of 75,000 years, higher fourth and fifth density helpers will arrive and support our ascension! Those of the same consciousness as Jesus when he was walking on Earth with us. And it is true! They are with us now! They surround our planet and each of us, as we make our CHOICE. Ra also shared that Jesus is now a fifth density being.

Why Create False Timelines?

If you were a predator whose main food was the Soul-force of a powerful race of beings on a powerful, unique planet, how would you devise to trap your prey and make sure you have a constant food and slave labor source? One way the Negative Aliens and their Cabal minions went about this was by fragmenting our natural timeline into multiple inverted reality pockets. They did this through well planned and timed traumatic catalytic events, which would then fragment human consciousness. They would then trap these Soul fragments into negative timeline loops. So, a person may be living 30% on the original timeline, and then have 35% captured in a negative timeline loop and another 35% in another negative loop. Some people leave the original timeline altogether and live completely in timeline fragments. I had a client once who would wake up in the morning with scratches and major bruises all up and down her arms. She lived alone with no pets. What had happened during the night to create this damage? When people are living on multiple timeline fragments, their physical body will show any marks or damage experienced by their other Soul fragments. Another example is when someone wakes up in the morning feeling like they didn't sleep at all. This is because once asleep, their consciousness goes into their body in another timeline and lives out that life. This could be an innate survival technique of the Mind-Body-Spirit, attempting to keep all parts from dying or becoming too damaged.

As we progress along our ascension journey, it is inevitable for all false timelines to collapse and dissolve. For ascension to happen, we and our planet must return fully to our true, divine timeline. Many clients and students have come to me seeking help with dealing with horrifying memories of torture and cataclysm not from this lifetime. They request a hypnotherapy session to explore the memories and play them out in more detail. Yet, the Higher Dimensional Helpers have guided me and my clients to recognize these memories are appearing now because the Soul parts from collapsing timelines are being liberated, and once they're free they are magnetically drawn back to the original Body-Mind-Spirit complex. Grand Master Qi, one of our Higher Dimensional friends, told us this:

"When these fragmented memories come it is your signal that a Soul part has made its way home from a false timeline where it was enslaved. Your job is to welcome it lovingly and have compassion for the trauma it has endured. That Soul part is not going to want to relive the trauma. Don't ask it to show you the details of that pain! What this Soul part needs is rest, care, and time to heal. That part needs to feel the difference between that world it left and this world, and that this world is safe and joyful. This will support your Soul parts in wanting to remain and being able to relax. Then, fill your life with joyful activities, people and places. This accelerates the healing process and allows for full integration. The focus needs to be on love and joy. This is the resonance of the original Divine Timeline. Do not try to recreate the traumatic false timeline loops! Why would you want to do that? Welcome your parts home into the Sacred! Let them remember who they are, that they are part of the Sacred. Then eventually, you will find that you are not fragmented anymore – you are One Whole Being again. Fourth Density will offer many joyful opportunities for this healing process."

Clarity Around the Popular Emphasis on 5D vs. 4D

The references to 5D Ascension began to flood the field starting in 2012. By 2016 I was enrolled in a 5D Business course, going to 5D conferences, and presenting on virtual 5D global summits. Then, I began reading the Law of One books and understanding more fully the relationship between dimensions and densities. I started asking myself, "what about 4D"? Why would we want to skip the Heart Chakra? Ra teaches that the negative polarity beings can ascend into 5D negative, skipping 4D and the lessons of Universal Love. But why would positive polarity Souls want to do this?

Later it came to me that those attracted to the 5D events were the Wanderers, whose home densities were at the 5th and 6th octaves. As years passed and the "5D" reference became more widely used in spiritual circles, those who are not Wanderers started getting confused. They started wondering about 4D and where does it fit in? I also noticed a strange spiritual bypass entering the field. Was 4th density too lame and the cool kids go straight to 5D? Remember Yeshua was a 4th density Soul at the highest level of that octave, who chose to travel from his Harmonic realm and enter into the reversal timeline of Earth to open up a Way back Home for us. His great sacrifice brought him into his 5th density ascension. So…have you mastered the lessons of Jesus Christ?

In 2020, I started hearing some spiritual guides on social media platforms describe 4D as ONLY the realm of negative demons and entities, like a negative astral plane. Here is where it gets confusing, because there is a difference between densities and dimensions. There can be many dimensions created within a density, depending on the Logoi of that Universe. There is a negative polarity 4th dimension within the 3rd density, where the malevolent disembodied entities and demons, etc., exist.

As far as densities go, every step on the path is necessary and relevant. We cannot skip Fourth Density. What if there was no F key on a piano?... The harmonic couldn't be realized. Because of all this confusion, I am going to lay out the clarity I've come to inner-stand, with the help of the Higher Dimensional Helpers.

As Planetary Ascension happens, which is now, the Wanderers will have many choices before them:

1. A 4th, 5th or 6th density Wanderer who has fully awakened to who they are will have an opportunity to be part of the transition team, supporting the third density communities of the planet to transition into fourth density structures and technologies. This Soul will remain in a denser Mind-Body-Spirit, yet arise into their true vibration of a unified consciousness. As well, they can now physicalize their multiple strands of DNA thereby reclaiming much of their higher dimensional abilities. These Wanderers may desire to serve as ambassadors, traveling to other planets as a representative of the Human Race, as Earth finally re-enters into the Galactic Community.
2. A 4th, 5th or 6th density Wanderer who has NOT fully awakened to who they are, and continues to struggle through the embedded traumas from the

enslavement of Earth, will have an opportunity to go at their own pace for awakening and healing. When they do fully remember, they will then be able to perceive higher choices before them.

3. A 5th density Wanderer has an opportunity to complete their 3D service mission and depart physical form. They can then choose to incarnate onto a 5th density planet with a 5th density Mind-Body-Spirit.

4. A 6th density Wanderer has an opportunity to depart their lower density physical form and return to their 6th density collective, taking on a light body once again.

Those people who are authentically Third Density Souls, and who make THE CHOICE for positive polarity, will naturally ascend into a Fourth Density positive timeline to begin learning the lessons of Universal Love. Most people will need time at the beginning of 4th density to detox from the insidious negative mind control we've endured, especially from an entrenched Perpetrator/Victim/Savior trauma-system. I perceive 4th density as being the journey of becoming Christed. Perhaps we will all have the honor to graduate from 4th density through an act of selfless service to a 3rd density planet, by opening a Way Home for them.

Now that our beautiful planet is liberated from the negative alien agenda, our 4th density timeline is destined for incredible greatness! I wouldn't be surprised if humanity reclaimed our planet's true name of Tara, or as some say, Terra.

CHAPTER 10

RETURN OF THE GALACTIC MOTHER

The planned fragmenting of our Souls for optimal enslavement and a consistent food source, also happened on a planetary level. Here's some information that may be painful and shocking, yet true...Our whole planet was derailed from her natural timeline and forced into a reversal matrix, regressing her evolution from 5D to 3D. For motivations of domination and immortality, this same negative faction in the Universe who preyed upon other solar systems before us, encased Tara (5D Earth) in a grid that is the reverse of our natural harmonic geometries or patterns of life, and blocked our connection to the Divine Mother Essence. The Harmonic Galactic Center is a powerful Mother Creator Consciousness, with which everything within the extended mass of the Milky Way galaxy should naturally be infused. Without the Divine Mother Essence anchored into the core of Earth, imbalance was inevitable. As we've been witnessing, the Father consciousness has been seduced from the harmonic grid and turned towards a service-to-self negative agenda. Dominance of a toxic patriarchal regime has engulfed the planet like wildfire.

The negative beings instigating this imbalance do not generate their own soul force, as they sacrificed their souls for a quest to become separate from The One Infinite Creator and attain immortality. Ergo they must feed off of the energy of other beings who do still have Soul-force. To make sure of a longer supply of this energy, they must stop the natural evolution of a planet. Our naturally accelerated journey through third density was thwarted; the planet has been stuck in several false time-loops, and was until recently, a feeding ground for these negative beings.

How did our planet become severed from the Divine Mother Essence at the core of our Milky Way Galaxy?

Information has come through Lisa Renee, galactic ambassador for Earth, that Earth once existed in a higher dimensional field, connected to the Divine Mother presence. In her Ascension Glossary, Lisa Rene describes the fifth density Earth, named Tara, which existed in the "second harmonic universe":

> Tara was attacked and exploded and imploded into a black hole. From the explosion, some of her fragments were pulled into lower densities, and became our 3D Solar System.

> The 5D planet Tara exploded millions of years ago and as a result, was sucked into a reversal black hole which fragmented the entire fifth dimensional planetary blueprint into 12 planetary bodies in our current third dimensional Solar System. This includes

the 3D version of Earth we inhabit in this Time Vector of the Universal Time Matrix. These 12 planets are Mercury, Venus, Earth, Mars, Maldek, Jupiter, Saturn, Uranus, Neptune, Pluto, Nibiru and then the Sun star.[12]

Given this account, our solar system was never linked to the Mother Essence in our current third density, because this is a reversal hologram galaxy. We were forced out of 5D, in a traumatic, violent way, into a false 3D reality matrix, where there is a finite-life black hole at the center of the galaxy. This severed our link to the eternal-life essence of the Eternal Universal Mother.

Not forever though!

Many of us have been incarnating into this reverse Earth thought-field with the specific mission to re-instate the Mother presence into our planet through awaking the Divine Mother star gates and using our own bodies as conduits for the transmissions from the eternal realms.

The Divine Mother is now entering full embodiment in our planet. Our galactic Logos is once again sending the

---

[12] https://ascensionglossary.com/index.php/Tara. Accessed on June 24, 2021.

constant in-streamings of Intelligent Energy from the center of the Milky Way.

Memories of Tara

Do you have memories of Tara?

Do you remember what it was like to move through your life with no fear for physical survival, knowing all your basic needs would always be met?

Do you remember what it was like to be witnessed by your community with love and value?

Do you remember what it was like to communicate with plants and animals telepathically?

Do you remember what it was like to be friends with many other beings from around the galaxy?

Do you remember your planet exploding...the disbelief...the horror?

Was it jarring for you to find yourself in the reversal hologram, where up was down and right was left, and you were blocked at every turn in remembering Tara?

Yes, me too.

Here's my story of remembering:

In 2018, Duane and I were staying at a friend's house in California. The house was up the hill from the Russian River, settled within a beautiful Redwood forest. Redwood trees are powerful conduits for cosmic information. It was mid-morning in the middle of winter, and everyone had gone out except me. I viscerally remember what happened next. I stoked the wood burning stove and sat down in an armchair to meditate. Without warning, I was suddenly out in space. A female being was hurling through space at me, mouth open in a scream, her energy body fractured. I reached out my arms to her and grabbed her as she flew by. I knew it was a part of me. My shamanic-mind told me this was a soul retrieval, though the part I was retrieving was not like any human being I'd ever seen. She was short and stalky and had a blue tinge to her skin. I held her and let her know she was now safe, and then I traveled with intension to my Over Soul. I experienced my Over Soul like a great radiant spiritual ball of light holding my individual Soul parts who are journeying in an out of incarnation in different realities and timelines. As I arrived in the pure radiant light of my Over Soul, I handed off this traumatized part of myself and trusted she would be tended back to wholeness.

After some integrative breathing, I relaxed again into meditation. Once again, without warning and suddenly, a being was standing before me. I recognized this being as an ally from the inner-Earth city of Telos on a parallel dimension within Mt. Shasta, California. The Telosians are "organic timeline protectors".

The being was telling me my presence was requested at Telos. I acknowledged and traveled instantaneously to a room deep within the Mountain. A circle of technicians was there waiting for my arrival. With my permission, they sat me in a strange looking chair with a helmet on it, which had a darkened glass-like shield that covered my eyes. They requested that I access the experience I'd just retrieved. I relaxed and the screen before my eyes became like a movie of a planet exploding. I was the small feminine being I'd retrieved, and I was living on the planet. The planet was way beyond 3D in consciousness and technology. There was no war, no military, no selfishness. Yet there were organized councils, including trade, and we were in relationship with planetary systems in many galaxies. Suddenly, the planet was exploding.

The Telosian technicians removed me from the helmet and chair and walked me over to a hologram hovering in the center of their standing circle. The hologram was a sphere. They requested I download all the information within me from the planet that exploded into their device. I don't know how, but I knew how to do this. I relaxed and emptied my mind. My eyelids started fluttering uncontrollably as a blue light streamed from my forehead into the center of the sphere, which was now clearly a hologram of the Earth. There was a green light at the core of the Earth, and through my help, a blue light was joining it. Together they seemed to be activating into a third energy.

Once this process completed, the Telosians thanked me. It seemed very important to them, but they wouldn't share the details with me. I was escorted back to the chair in my friend's house. I opened my eyes. What had just happened? Then, my researcher-mind jumped into action. I went to my computer to look up exploding planets. I had known about Lisa Rene's Ascension Glossary from a couple friends, but never personally explored it. Something in me knew I would find answers there about this exploding planet. Once on the site, I searched for "exploding planet." Up came the pages for "The Souls of Tara," and Tiamat. I read everything I could find; my whole body was coursing with energy. If I had read the story about Tara before my own remembering of the event, I could have easily chalked my visions up to this previous knowledge. Because I had such a powerful, full-body remembering and then found information to back it up, I am of the opinion that something like what Lisa Rene reports is indeed true. So, since the timeline reversal, when Tara exploded and was sent through a reverse timeline black hole, the Earth's natural harmonic has been blocked.

After the reversals and creation of false timelines, humanity fell deeper into confusion, chaos and fear, trapping them in the material reality of 3D. The severance from Soul, Nature, the Feminine, and Universal Law allowed those vying for "power over" to gain more control and deepen the illusion further through, as I laid out earlier, individual Soul capture and creation of multiple fragments, then dispersal on multiple negative timeline loops. The term "loops" refers to the evil design of endlessly sling-shotting the Soul fragment into forced reincarnation within the negative timeline they died within.

Humanity has been struggling through the false-timelines on Earth for millennia, manipulated and herded towards enslavement, all the while continuing to seek freedom, truth, and love. Multi-generational trauma has embedded fear into our neurology, cells, and DNA until we've become addicted to negative emotions and chaotic systems. Our planet's strongholds of harmonic grids, vortices, and cultures protecting the truth have almost all been hunted down and harnessed for the negative agenda or destroyed. The Wanderers continue to come, clearing portals, anchoring in Ascension Codes and preparing humanity for the inevitable liberation.

Over the past 200 years, the numbers of Wanderers have exponentially increased. The social movements to break down divides and rally for sovereignty have also increased each decade. Beginning in the new millennia, our year 2000, Indigenous elders from tribes around the world began traveling from their remote villages to speak to the public about the great shift; sharing their star knowledge and prophesies.

As well, a Way Home was opened and assured by the incarnation of the Galactic Mind, Yeshua, onto Earth. This was his whole mission and purpose. Once accomplished, this pathway home to 5th Density could never be hidden or destroyed. Anyone who sincerely sought for it would find it. Even with the ensuing confusion and rewriting of Yeshua's life story, they could never change the power of his teachings and light. Many other teachers came before him to prepare the Field for his mission to be fulfilled; and came after him to ensure the protection of his message and to further widen access to the Way Home.

We now witness negative groups grasping onto their last remnants of power, yet there is nothing they can do to turn the tide. Ascension is inevitable. False timelines are now dissolved. More and more people perceive the Way Home and are choosing to walk this path to peace and harmony.

CHAPTER 11

RETURN OF THE AWAKENED FATHER

Men have been used as pawns in a power-game by global elite bankers and royals who play both sides of every war, which they designed and then implemented. If men won't be their soldiers, then they are refused their masculinity and dumbed down so they don't ask questions. The fierce loyalty, huge compassion and joyful laughter of our men has been missing for centuries and the pain of this non-expression has taken them into addictions, guilt, self-hatred and suicide.

Survival for men in this "woke" culture has been to sever from their physicality and passion and become puppets of A.I. or to overly-feminize[13] and lose their ability to defend and protect. I, as a woman, desire men to know

---

[13] I am speaking here of the intentional negative agenda to weaken men through pushing a feminizing campaign onto and into them. I am not judging, in any way, anyone's authentic experience of their inner-polarities or sexual orientation.

how sacred they are. I, as a woman, desire men to break free from enslavement.

Yes, the Great Mother is back and she's pissed. But just wait! Because when the Divine Masculine wakes up...Evil has No Chance!!

Beloved Men, you are needed, loved and desired!

YANG RISING TO CLEAR THE FIELD

October 7, 2021

FROM GRAND MASTER QI:

There is sometimes a moment...a moment along the timeline, we look at it now in a linear way, as if you are walking along a path. Sometimes on the path you walk upon, there is a chasm; A very dangerous part, yes? As if your path is suddenly along a very steep cliff and the path is very narrow and you have to skirt along the edge and the path crumbles, yes? And this is always a moment where there is a great test that you face. It is an internal test. It is a test of your courage. It is a test of your faith. Specifically- your faith in yourself and a Greater Power that holds you, and is you. It is a test of your trust in all that is good around you, and that you are deeply loved and held. There are many ways we could describe this test, but you understand what we get at here.

Therefore, on this point of the journey you face a test and at first, when you first perceive this juncture on the road, first thought that appears is doubt, OK, first thought is doubt. Because you've never experienced your capacity to face such a test. It has never appeared in your life before. There has never been such motivation to face something this dangerous. What you perceive to be dangerous, yes? But, actually not dangerous at all, it is all in how you perceive things, yet it is necessary to perceive the danger, you see because it is in relationship with the motivation. You must have the danger, the perception of danger or risk, that catalyzes your volition...your...you could say, aggressive nature, or better word would be your assertive-Yang nature. You have to get that yang fiery nature ignited within you. The warrior must come forward, because that yang principle within yourself, this consciousness, this is the part which is going to give you the energy, give you the inner-knowing and confidence...Confidence is not right word, it is too small for what I describe, but you know what I mean, ...to make that leap over the chasm, or to face that danger or take that risk, OK.

Therefor the passive, which is the Yin... Sometimes you get into a yin cycle, where it is easier to be passive and let life happen to you and just going with the routine because it is easier to not rock the boat. Therefore, the yang principle becomes suppressed within you...dampened, yes, within you. It takes a great igniting, something very big to ignite the yang coming back to life. And therefore, it takes...for the yang... you say, for the male-aspect...The male-aspect who is in despair because he feels unneeded, OK, he feels unneeded, unwanted, not good enough, he is in his wounded heart and feels very wounded, because the feminine, yes, the inner-female, has lost herself. She has forgotten who she is. She has become identified solely from the external world, telling her who she is, what she is supposed to be, have, do, etc. And she has taken her cues from the outside world for so long that she has forgotten that she has an inner-male who she needs. She needs him to pierce through illusion and come back to the inner-Universe, yes, that is more real. Therefore, the feminine must be experiencing severe heartache and suffering for the masculine to pop out of his own dullness. He will do anything for her. He will do anything for her. Yet, if she does not need him, he feels useless. Suddenly, he feels a ping in his heart. The ping gets stronger and stronger...becomes louder and louder. Suddenly his ears come out of the dullness and he can hear her cry. Suddenly his heart becomes a blazing fire. His lingam becomes very hard. He rises up and he feels all of his pure longing and desire to be with her. And if she is suffering...he will not have it. Right? He must get activated to this point...and her calling out to him is what it takes. Her remembering there is something more and praying sincerely and calling out for help. He will respond, yes, he is the hero. He is stimulated by nothing else...Her call for him is IT! So, he jumps up, out of all the doldrums and the great waves begin to form on the ocean. He becomes all of the great gods of all of your old myths: Thor, he becomes Poseidon...he becomes these massive presences of the masculine and this is his true nature. He comes in to change reality for her. He comes in to support her. To have her expression that is her true expression. He does not rescue her. Yes, it is not about rescuing. He comes to clear the field. He comes to clear the mind, OK. He is the lord over the mind. She is the queen of creativity and energy, yes, in the womb and second chakra. Therefore together, he helps connect her again to her true power in spirit. And her presence in his life helps connect him once again to his root, and connection to Gaia and nature and his intuition. And so, all of this happens at once when they come into each other's lives again.

OK, so, this is a very dramatic story...

But is necessary to tell you because this is context for what you are experiencing now...

For you are jumping!

You are facing the test and you are right in mid-leap over that chasm.

You called in your masculine and together you have the power to do what you need to do right now.

In many, many ways, this juncture in your timeline, this point of your inner and outer world, it is the beginning of a congruency between the two that you have yet experienced the harmonizing of...your inner and outer is imperative, it is the most important thing right now. For you were facing the true, true danger was not the fear of jumping the chasm and all that comes up for you around that. The true danger would be to not do anything... and become schizoid. You would have been like a person chopping wood, and you split the wood, you would have split like this, it would have been a loud crack in your psyche. You would be feeling the pain of the crack that starts small but then gets deeper, deeper...yes... you would have felt the intensity of the cracking of your psyche. For there is a point of no return when you abandon and abandon, yes. We are not saying that your life has not been courageous. For your life has been of course sacred all the way through. Each test you face is the test for that moment. This test you are in now could not have come at any earlier time. Yet, this was the greatest test because you were facing a very great danger of a split.

Therefore, as you perceive currently in your mind-body-spirit, the choice you have made...for you were fighting for your life... and that is the greatest motivation to leap over what seems like an insurmountable chasm.

Yet, you have leapt!

(End Transmission)

The arising of the Divine Mother and Divine Father is at hand. These two powerful forces within us, awakened in love and ready to participate, allow us to tap into Universal Creative potential and energies never before accessed. This is exactly what must happen to complete the re-integration of our fragments and simultaneously the re-integration of our planet's fragments. It takes work and focus, yes! But why else did we come here?

It's a New Time, my friends!

Don't expect reality to react in old ways to your New Consciousness. This is our moment. Let's see what we're capable of!

CHAPTER 12

OUR ORGANIC TIMELINE IS ASSURED

Let's dive into some "disclosure movement" information to further connect the dots and strengthen our comprehension of timelines and current events.

Project Looking Glass

Project Looking Glass is a top secret technological device, brought to Earth by a more advanced extra-terrestrial race. It was first in the hands of the U.S. military, and then somehow ended up in the hands of the globalist elite. This device is something like, but I'm not sure of the details, a reverse-engineered Pineal Gland! Yes, you read that right.

Our Pineal Gland is the endocrine gland located in the center of our brains. It's shaped like an upside-down pine cone. It is filled with water on the inside, and has rod and cone cells, exactly the same kind of cells in our eyes, on the interior walls. Inside the fluid of the pineal gland there are DMT crystals. What are those? DMT stands for

Dimethyltryptamine. This is a psychedelic chemical found naturally in plants, animals and our pineal gland! DMT is activated by consciousness and can receive transmissions of information from higher dimensions or quantum levels of reality. (I experience strong pineal gland activity while I'm channeling, with streams of visions, colors, geometries, etc., which always correlate to the messages being given by the Higher Dimensional Helpers). Also, our pineal glands are coated with cells on the outside that protect it from electro-magnetic interference and radiation. It's a sealed chamber in our brains that quite literally is an inner-eye! So, imagine a piece of advanced technology that can act like an inner-eye, able to tap into imagery from possible future timelines for our planet?

The device used in Project Looking Glass enabled users to perceive these possible futures and offered them an advantage over positive alliances working for freedom. You can imagine, this can be used for good or bad. The Globalist Elite backed by the Negative Alien agenda, used it to plot their course for world domination and depopulation of 80% of humanity. Depopulation would require well planned and timed global cataclysms which would then ensure a future of multi-generational trauma, and thus continued easy capture of Soul fragments into false timeline loops.

But then something happened...

Around 2010 the device showed members of the globalist elite, that at winter solstice in the year 2012, all possible timelines suddenly converge into just one. Instead of being able to choose the timeline that best suited their agenda, they were given only one option now, and it wasn't in their favor. I see this as yet more proof that 2012 was a powerful gateway year into a golden age for our planet!

A further confirmation of this information came through Laura Eisenhower during her three-hour Webinar in March 2020. She reported that "the years 2010 through 2012 were a predestined time period for the end of the "service-to-self", false timelines and the "return of the Cosmic Aether"", AKA the fifth element.[14]

The Awakening is At Hand

The Higher Dimensional Helpers told Duane and I on May 14 of 2020 that the harder the negative factions try, the more they will fail...and that an event will come soon that will activate the people of Earth.

THE AWAKENING IS AT HAND

May 14, 2020

COUNCIL OF FIFTY SPEAKS: We greet you in the love and the light of the Infinite Creator. May our

---

[14] To connect more to Laura Eisenhower's work go to https://cosmicgaia.org/. This quote access in March 2020.

voices find your voice in aligned frequency and pure tone.

There are messages that must be relayed to you now:

The time is coming close for the people to rise up and claim their right to the Law of One and Sovereignty. There is a time that is coming soon, where the Souls of the deceased will return in their light-bodies to stand by the side of the living to fortify their strength, determination and essence.

(Vision of protests).

The voice of the people will rise to deafening volume.

The ones of deception, who have severed from their Souls in grandiosity with an agenda to rule over your planet, are completing their catalytic work, having served their purpose. Playing the role of the "deep and dark" and the people's choice will be made.

The awakening is at hand.

We sense the heart field of humanity at this time and gauge their desire to respond. Their premonitions, their foreboding We foresee in the field the momentum, we would say, the energy to leap is building within the people.

The imagining of the leap is preparing them for the leap. And soon a catalyst so great will come there will be no thought just action, just the leap, just the Yes to Love. We cannot tell you the specifics of this catalyst. Just know that a great light is coming. A great light will infuse and animate all upon the planet. And what you call mind-control structures will incinerate away. (Image of people coming out of disillusionment).

The hearts of the people will cry out for justice.

The children are activated. Around the planet they are the conduits for the pure light of the One – The New Gaia Vibration of Love. They're anchoring it into Gaia, every day, now through their innocence and trust, through their pure hearts. Your greatest ally, in collective humanity, now and as it has always been, The Children.

GREAT MOTHER DRAGON COUNCIL SPEAKS:

Dear Ones, The Rose Pink ray gathers in your heart to ease your fears. Lay yourself in the hands of the Mother. Connect with the Sun and replenish. We are the Dragon council. We are Dragonkind. We are an emanation of the Great Mother Presence. We protect this planet. We watch over creation. We watch over all creatures. We watch over the evolutionary journey of all life, form, existence, and expression. The consciousness and the mind of the planet is purifying. And so, the mind of the beings upon the planet purify. The mind enters into a crystallized state of clarity and stillness and a knowing of truth beyond truth.

The games of pretend played by children to explore what it is to be other than yourself are over in the consciousness of humanity. The adult consciousness must initiate now. You must go through the portal and see yourselves clearly. There are millions, billions, countless guardians and allies with you. Your fear and suffering come from forgetting this. Feel joy and rise up.

You hold the bridge strong for those preparing to leap. We are with you. Break Free. Know Yourself.

DUANE: How are the Higher Dimensional Allies supporting us right now?

DRAGON COUNCIL: We gather with you daily. Our interactions with humanity does not falter. It is our commitment to you; each one of you.

Whatever you call us, we are emanations of the One.

The Alliance, as you call them, is more than just one grouping. The Alliance you could say are like many pods who can come together in a super pod, just like your dolphins. The Alliance is working from many angles on many dimensions. The Alliance is even time-traveling at this time, to open up portals of density and clear them, that the Mother Love-Light may not get lost.

There is a timeline war happening and many are traveling back to shift the timeline away from the inevitable in this particular timeline. Yet, those who would try to thwart the timeline away from Ascension will fail over and over again. And each time they attempt it, they ensure their own demise in the present timeline. They tighten the noose so to speak. This is simply because it is their time to die, and they're choosing not to. It is only weakening them, their resistance.

The health and the vibrancy of Gaia and humanity is at such a strength and only growing stronger. It is the people connected that strengthens the field and you strengthen each other. The pockets of fear, doubt, and suffering will be infiltrated by the love of neighbors and friends and global meditators.

In your United States, there are many players involved in power struggles. There are many agendas. There is the financial agenda. There is the capitalist agenda. There is the spiritual agenda, and there are thousands of spiritual agendas. There is the environmental agenda. There is the technological agenda. Each one taking steps to grab power and feed their agenda.

The agendas themselves are ideas of what would be ultimate fulfillment. And these ideas have taken on a life of their own, like crying, insatiable babies that must be constantly fed. Yet it is all an illusion. When you drop the agendas you are closer to the truth of who you are and what you are and what you are capable of. So many are unable to make the leap quite yet, to understand how powerful they are in just their pure consciousness-ability to turn light and sound into new creation.

But this will come. You must be patient.

We speak now to you who remember these realms of creation and freedom: You may wish to be there now because being here is too painful. But remember, this is not your world, it is theirs (present time humanity). You chose to come here to serve. It is the end of their enslavement. You must find ways to resource yourselves and remember that you are not of this place, yet you are here. So remember you are Free Now and that these agendas do not impact you, though you may think they do.

The agendas are constantly changing and the inevitable journey is for the diverse singular agendas to meet each other in negotiation and to a new harmonic that serves all life. It may take time for this to happen, as there are many diverse opinions, yet it will come as the field lightens on your planet.

DUANE: What is the likelihood of the Cabal players being arrested?

DRAGON COUNCIL: You know, even these beings are playing such an extreme game of pain. They are playing pretend and they have pretended for so long that they believe it is true. Yet their over-Soul continues to be available to them.

Even if they choose the negative path, they will never be able to sever themselves from the One. It's impossible. Therefore, when you think of them or say their names continue to see them infused with love, connected to Source, and awakening. Hold them in love. Let go of your attachment to their punishment. Unplug from this whole paradigm and see them free from suffering. See them liberated from the negativity and the suffering of being severed from their Souls.

Even if they reject it, because it is not the food they choose to eat at this time, they will become so tired when the fear levels drop on the planet and there is less to feed on and there are no more captive children to terrorize, their negative helpers will abandon them as useless. Many will pass away and transition to go through a very profound recalibration within their own universe. And others will defiantly pretend they don't need anyone else and try to generate their own terror/food, which will fail. Send them love.

CLOSING MESSAGE FROM THE DRAGON COUNCIL: See your world infused in love every day. Use your power, the power of Love, to infuse your planet. Let love guide you and let go of wanting to know. For the wanting to know comes from fear of losing control. Fear of your rights being taken away. Fear of losing your sovereignty. Fear of losing each other. The fear feeds the negative. Those who feed off fear grow stronger. Therefore, focus on Love and let go of needing to know what happens next, for Love will guide you.

Participate with no animosity in the changing of these times. Your role is not to point fingers, to judge, to hate. Your role is to stay the vibration and keep it as high as possible for yourself and for the world. So that this transition can be as smooth as possible. You are with hundreds of thousands of Lightworkers, Lightbringers, and Starseeds doing this together.

And so it is.

(End of Transmission)

Ascension into the unified field of Fourth Density requires 51% of a person's consciousness to have chosen love. Those who choose the negative polarity will not be ascending. And those who resist the transformation, and do not make a choice either way, will incarnate into another 75,000-year grand cycle of third density on another third-density planet, with opportunities for Harvest every 25,000 years. They can take as many lifetimes as they need to make their choice.

Do the choices and actions of the Lightworkers who are ascending impact those who are still in chaos? Have you heard of the Hundredth Monkey theory? It is relevant here. Basically, after a certain number of beings in a certain species makes an adaptation or takes a leap in consciousness, the new consciousness and behaviors suddenly appear in the rest of the species, no matter where they are in the world. I have been noticing that the consciousness of humanity around the world is shifting towards a striving for truth, even if it's uncomfortable, rather than continuing on in fear or an "ignorance is bliss" mentality.

REMEMBER:

We are crystallizing the lessons of the Third Density. These are the lessons about power and love of others, realizing we're all One. This embodied wisdom comes over lifetimes of self-work and an unceasing commitment to Love. Because we are all connected at the Quantum level of existence and are made up of the same Source consciousness, and because Love is the strongest force in the

Universe, even one person popping open into Unity Consciousness will impact all people. Imagine the power of millions of people waking up! Or a billion!

CHAPTER 13

ASCENSION HAPPENS LIKE CLOCKWORK

During a channeling session Duane and I held on July 9th of 2019, the Higher Dimensional Helpers told us that to ascend, we must attain a surrendered state of self-love and self-acceptance and an equal level of love and acceptance for others, with no judgements. This is also known as a state of unconditional love and acceptance, which comes from self-knowledge and embodied wisdom. It is this quality of vibration that liberates us from the reversal grids and distortions.

What are you doing in your life to further develop this state in yourself? It's a humbling question.

Here is an offering on this subject from my Star Family:

TIMELINES, ASCENSION, AND THE REUNION IN 6D

January 9, 2020

DUANE: Can you describe further about Project Looking Glass, which is a device that the secret government or Cabal, have used to look at possible timelines for our planet, so they can manipulate the masses to achieve the outcome that benefits them the most. We heard through insider Bill Woods, that as 2012 was approaching, the Cabal was getting scared because every time they tried to use Looking Glass, it now was showing that on Dec. 21, 2012, all possible timelines for the Earth converged into just one timeline. And the one timeline wasn't in their favor at all, because it's what we might call the Ascension experience. Can you say more about this?

PLEIADIAN COUNCIL: As you know and have acknowledged, ascension is inevitable. Evolution happens. It is folly for those who would assert power-over and enslave, or try to enslave, consciousness itself, within one reality sphere eternally, for their own benefit. It is folly. It is simply showing the growth state of those who would pretend this could happen. This is the Creator Source choosing to explore herself through the experience of wanting something it cannot have and the extremes of denial consciousness - the extremes of service to self, in your dimension, upon your planet. The laws of the Universe are the laws of the Universe. They cannot be changed. Just as the laws of physics on your planet are the laws of physics on your planet. The exploration is the exploration. Certain beings will push it to the limit. And this is another expression of the One. The diversification of consciousness to the extremes of polarity. Yet all are particles of the One. And there can be no other truth. This is Divine Law. The Law of One.

And so, the timeline, it has come to the point where all of the timelines converge upon one timeline that leads to the Harvest. For all third dimensional planets and material experiences, this point happens. It happens when the diversification reaches an extent, that is stretched as far as it can stretch. Like a rubber band, yes? And then it flings back in on itself, becoming a singular path. A choice is made by each being. You would not have incarnated at this time, unless you already knew your answer.

Even those who feel confused and exhibit chaotic consciousness, bouncing back and forth, even they, in their heart of hearts have already chosen. And when the time comes and the catalytic pressure is on, it will be easy to step across the threshold. Meaning it will be easy to know who they are and what they're not. For all children dabble in wrong-doing, to explore what they're not. Name-calling, punching someone, lighting something on fire, killing frogs... And yet, in the end, as the being grows, they cease with these behaviors as they find new behaviors that bring much more fulfillment such as open-heartedness and connection. These meet their needs far and beyond more than what enacting what they are NOT could have ever gotten them.

For some souls who are drunk on power and self-gratification, it will take multiple dimensional incarnations for them to fully explore the service-to-self polarity, and then they will also give it up, of their own free will choice, to enter into Universal Love. And to have the ecstatic moment of homecoming into the heart of the One. Embraced in the arms of all those who chose positive polarity consistently. These homecomings are most profound and celebrated in the sixth density, as all who are lost and all who strayed, no matter how long it takes them, do make it back to source, back to truth.

The power of this reunion in sixth density is beyond anything else experienced up to that point, as far as LOVE, and the experience of love is concerned. The reunion of the negative and positive polarities is the ultimate reunion. The ultimate sacred marriage of truest love. Return to each other, after so long apart; the wholeness attained. The Christ consciousness attained together as they now journey as one towards 7th density.

And so, as you are yet in third density, though it is the close of this density upon your world, though you may view these beings who assert control and continue to manipulate and to harm children, as evil, these are the very souls who in sixth density, you will be wrapping your arms around in the high octave of Joy, that your true love has come home.

This is the internal journey of all and the external journey of all.

We acknowledge that in all things exists the Law of One - the magnetic pull of Source. All is always being gathered into wholeness again.

(End of Transmission)

Proof of Ascension in Our Planet's Past

Many metaphysicians, visionaries, archeologists and channels before me have gone deep into this vast subject and published books or made documentaries. It is not within my own expertise, though I am very curious about it.

There is proof beyond a doubt that planet Earth has gone through many cycles of renewal throughout the epochs and ages, including two full pole shifts. Besides the extensive mentions of this in almost every ancient culture's calendrical accounts, there have also been amazing discoveries around the world of unexplainable under-ocean ruins of what seem to be advanced civilizations. Lemuria, Mu and Atlantis are the most famous of these former-cycle civilizations. The Higher Dimensional Helpers told me in 2019 that during the time of Lemuria there were nine great civilizations thriving on the planet.

In most of the ancient calendrical records that still exist, you can find reference to a great flood. The oldest known is the Mesopotamian Sumerian Flood Story, also known as the Eridu Genesis. [15] This flood story is retold in ancient Babylon, ancient Egypt and then with Noah and the Ark in the old testament of the Bible. Lisa Renee received a timeline from her Helpers in which they state there was a flood that took out Atlantis, which occurred 11,500 years ago.[16] And the Law of One material refers to the final sinking of Atlantis 9,600 years ago.[17] Clearly, there was a massive sea-level rise, perhaps storms too, which impacted the planet's civilizations of that time severely. Now, we have new disclosure of a more recent global cataclysm which created mud floods which buried many major cities around the world. Previously hidden archives with photographs are being released out of Russia, showing hundreds of people digging out cities from 10 to 20 feet of mud. Why don't we know about this? Don't worry, we will. The years to come will be full of disclosure of our true history and heritage.

---

[15] https://brewminate.com/eridu-genesis-the-sumerian-and-oldest-flood-story-in-ancient-texts/. Accessed on June 23, 2021.

[16] https://ascensionglossary.com/index.php/Historical_Timeline_Trigger_Events. Accessed on June 23, 2021.

[17] www.lawofone.info/timeline.php. Accessed on June 23, 2021.

According to Ra, opportunities for Harvest occur every 25,000 years and then at the close of the grand cycle. Ra shares in the transmissions that 50,000 years ago there was an end to a "Major Cycle 1" and there was no Harvest. At that time the average lifespan was 700 years. Then 25,000 years ago was the end of "Major Cycle 2" and again, there was no harvest. The average lifespan on Earth was 35-100 years. "…although one South American group was 4D+ harvestable but chose to remain in 3D", explains Ra. As for our current opportunity for Harvest, Ra expressed it would be sometime around NOW. And, Ra shared that the full transition from third density into fourth density could last until 2681 AD.[18] This makes sense to me, considering that Fourth Density can last up to thirty-million Earth years.

When we back up and perceive these vaster cycles of creation and growth, it can certainly shift how we relate to our current human experience, can't it? How long have we been returning to grow, learn, teach, and serve? How many major Soul lessons have we worked on to get to where we are today? If you are a Wanderer, you may be wondering, "How old am I?"

One thing that I have to keep reminding myself is that it's not about me (ego) and what that small me wants. Our negatively manipulated minds and cultures live in a false experience of time that is very confusing. We are either

---

[18] www.lawofone.info/timeline.php. Accessed on June 23, 2021.

running away from something, or running towards something, always anxious and impatient, wanting instant gratification. We have been herded away from our Wisdom, Grace, Centeredness, and Sovereignty, through carefully designed seductive pathways built into our movies, video games, TV shows, social media, internet and smart phones. My point being, when I tell people that the work we do today will liberate the Divine Soul of Humanity and anchor the Divine Mother geometries back into our planet, and 100 years from now our descendants will be living the fruits of our labors, people get disappointed because they want that amazing reality right now for themselves. And, of course, I do too! It's been a challenging reality so far, to say the least!

My encouragement is:

Can you give your heart fully into your immediate service?

Can you remember why you chose your current mission?

Can you stay devoted to the larger collective mission?

That said, remember, we are on the "eve of rapid transformation". Because we have been blocked from natural ascension we've been in an unnatural arrested development. Once that block is removed, WHICH IT IS NOW, our human race is going to take off like a horse onto a wide open field! We have a LOT of catching up to do.

The benevolent E.T.'s and positive polarity Taran councils with Space Force, will be time-releasing advanced technology and disclosing our true heritage and history in a way that won't overwhelm or shock us. Yet, we literally are launching into a Star Trek future! Think of it as an honor to be on the "transition team", as Alex Collier, Andromedan Contactee[19], puts it! Time to roll up our sleeves and be the ancestors who will be remembered for our strength, resiliency, courage, vision and unshakable love. (This last paragraph added on January 1, 2022).

------

[19] Sourced from the December 31, 2021 Q&A Webinar on January 1, 2022. www.alexcollier.org

CHAPTER 14

ENDING CYCLES OF REPEATED HISTORY

The Ascended Giants of the Yucatan Peninsula

I want to share a deeply profound encounter Duane and I had with an ascended group of beings from the village of Kohunlich in the Yucatan peninsula of Mexico. These beautiful, gentle beings told us their ascension experience and offered us clarity and encouragement for our current journey. I am also going to share some related research that I feel amazingly correlates and supports the transmissions we received.

In October of 2019, Duane, our apprentice Danielle, and I were traveling for our second year in a row through the Yucatan doing repair and activation lightwork on the energetic grids and vortexes. In this work, we experience ourselves like acupuncture needles, channeling Love-Light from the Harmonic Field through our bodies and into the specific locations where we're called to serve. This helps to clear the embedded miasms of trauma, frozen timeline events, and negative "spells" or "curses", just like clearing stagnant or blocked chi in our bodies during an acupuncture treatment. Anyway, this particular day we all agreed our work lay at the ruins of Kohunlich, near the border of Belize.

The minute we set foot on the grounds we knew the location was protected in the positive polarity and a higher vibrational field. The ruins were phenomenal and jaw-dropping! The detail of the stone carving at the Temple of the Masks was otherworldly and clearly full of light-codes. We found a sunny place to sit and opened to a transmission from the ascended ancestors of that place. Linking to them happened almost immediately and easily for us. They were grateful and even joyful to connect.

Our questions were around their ascension experience. Clearly, they built these structures and lived there in Kohunlich, yet the cities were abandoned at some point. Why? As well, to our eyes, observing the structures, we felt there were two different races living together, one of giants and one of shorter statured beings. Some of the buildings had steps that were around twenty-inches in height, and very challenging to go up for regular people, while other buildings had shorter steps, around 5 to 6-inches in height.

Just the year before the three of us had been exploring and channeling in the Mayan ruins of Palenque, in the state of Chiapas, Mexico. The information we gathered during that trip was part of what propelled us in Kohunlich. We had met a local who had been part of the original team who discovered the ruins of Palenque, in the 1950's. We took this gem of an elder to lunch, and everyone we ran into treated him with great respect. The restaurant owner even gave him his lunch for free! This man told us that when the remains of King Pakal were found, they were in a ten-foot long sarcophagus and his skull was elongated in the back. He also had nine Chinese jade bracelets on one wrist. King Pakal was believed to be the most powerful king to rule in the region during the seventh century.

While writing this, Duane just found an article from the Washington Post from 2014, which reports that it was the French archaeologist Alberto Ruz Lhuillier who discovered the hidden tomb room of King Pakal, after four years of digging with his team. He took images of the elaborate carvings on Pakal's sarcophagus lid which seem to depict him wearing special clothing, sitting in some sort of craft related to astronomy, star gazing, star navigating, or space travel.[20]

The elder we took to lunch told us the buildings of Palenque were originally covered with symbols similar to many ancient cultures known today, including Hebrew menorahs, Egyptian hieroglyphs, and Chinese dragons. He said he remembered how the scientist commanded all these

---

[20] Washington Post article written by Maya Kroth, June 12, 2014. Accessed online on June 25, 2021. A web link for this article can be found in the Resources section.

symbols carved off the stones before the location became a national park in the 1980's and opened to the public.

This man also shared with us that he had been shown in seven dreams how the Egyptians and Mayans were able to travel between the Giza plateau and Palenque. They had flying crafts. Before I leave the topic of this gem of an elder and Palenque, I'll tell one more story from him. He said that just one year before he had met a farmer who lived on the outskirts of the town of Palenque. This man had been digging on his land one day and found a sink hole. He and his son opened it up and climbed in. They discovered bones! Very large bones. Too long to be the bones of modern day humans. And they found a giant elongated skull. For this part of the book I hopped onto my laptop to research our Giant Ancestors and found an article on Gaia.com with proof that the Smithsonian Institute has destroyed the bones of giant humanoids, which had been sent to them from across America, since the early 1900's.

The Palenque stories are a good preface to what happened for us the following year in 2019, encountering the ascended Maya of Kohunlich. This transmission from Kohunlich, to read it now, blows my mind! It sounds like and feels like they were preparing us for the events that were about to take place starting in the Fall of 2019, and spanning through 2020 and 2021. They gave us the information we needed through telling their own stories, never breaking any Universal Laws by giving us too much information that might influence our own organic responses to current events. In the

Law of One, Ra calls this the Law of Confusion, which is also called the Law of Free Will. [21] Sometimes, the Higher Dimensional Helpers cannot share certain events or information with us, even if they may want to.

Here is what they shared:

CHANNELING FROM KOHUNLICH RUINS, MEXICO

October 23, 2018

ASCENDED BEINGS OF KOHUNLICH: We greet you with rainbows.

It is very different here from the perception of your bodies and eyes... to feel the air...to perceive the jungle...

And these ruins of what was once our village...our home...

Very many descendants are still here.

(Interruption)

There was much life here that was shared.

---

[21] https://www.lawofone.info/results.php?q=law+of+confusion. From transmission 3.14. Accessed on June 25, 2021.

We would say that it is right and good for civilizations to fall.

This [skeleton/ruins] is just what is left of the "body"... the structures that held the pulsing heart and soul of the people's consciousness...and we grew out of it.

You are seeing old forms of how we used to build with the matter from the earth. In this realm it is easy to take for granted material supply. There can be a coveting of certain molecular configurations such as the Jade or Obsidian, and the Gold.

When your species moves beyond into the crystalline matrix there is no coveting anymore, because everything you need is what you are, and that is Consciousness. That is the value: The evolving and the expanding of your own consciousness.

Perceiving the light matrices that connect everything in their beauty...This is great accomplishment on the journey for higher dimensional life. The children strive to be able to perceive the beauty and the geometry all around them. We live in the light.

We, many of us, ascended to a city of light constructed by our consciousness through our good deeds while we were here in this dimension. Just as you are doing now, creating temples of light, cities of light, harmonics, ... ways of being and living together, with all of your good deeds.

You are striving for awakening.

There is so much that we would like to share with you. Our technologies have advanced to the point of healing instantaneously. We spend so much of our time now in service and also creating beauty and art. There is no need to spend time on survival. There is no fear.

What we value most greatly is the children. They are our greatest joy. Everyone wants to spend time with them.

(Interruption)

We are willing to answer questions...

DUANE: One of those beings that was depicted on the Temple of the Masks said that the way to their realm is through love, through Mas Amor.

What were some of the steps you took to bring yourself into this enlightened state from this third density world, to where you are now?

ASCENDED BEINGS OF KOHUNLICH: Just as you are in communion with us now, we were in communion with higher dimensional support systems as well. They informed us of the coming changes. Of the coming contractions in consciousness, of a great dark cloud that would move through the consciousness of humanity and darken the light.

We saw what was to come in visions through the ceremonies with the plants and mushrooms, and [through] our communion with [the] higher dimensions.

(Pause)

We of course were not like you, but of a different genetic strain, much taller than you.

DUANE: Thus, the huge steps!

ASCENDED BEINGS OF KOHUNLICH: We came up from South America. There was a great pilgrimage from Peru, and the cities of gold and light there. We came, not on foot, but through the portal systems and crafts, [to arrive] here.

It was a time of experimentation [on Earth]...a time of, you could say, territorial land grabbing...in the beginning.

And then, through the generations much of this was forgotten or was just legend that was revered and used to teach the children. We started losing our intelligence around our beginnings. Our pineal glands began to get smaller. We began working with the [sacred psychedelic mushrooms and] plants to help us understand. We saw that the time of complete forgetting was coming. And that in that digression there would be factions that would take advantage.

Maria is asking if this digression was a natural organic process or if it was manipulated?

ASCENDED BEINGS OF KOHUNLICH: It is difficult to explain at the level that you can understand, how many pieces,… how many groups, were invested.

We wanted to live in peace. We left the experiments. We wanted to be independent and sovereign, and grow of our own accord.

For we were a hybridization, yes, of three different races. We love this planet and chose to be here to raise our children. To live simply.

Yet, by the time the [great, dark] cloud came, the illusion began to seep through the consciousness of the people all over [the lands]. We were already so far removed from our ancestors who migrated North, that it was hard for us to relate to that time and reasoning. So, when we had access to [the] influence of, [who] we perceived, [were] more intelligent beings and societies…

(Interruption)

So, those who were keeping the wisdom tried to continue the holding of everyone [in Kohunlich], in [the awakened] consciousness, and [the] sharing [of] the visions. It's very difficult when you're in that position to not manipulate to keep people safe. When you see that other factions are using manipulation, yet, you want your people to be free and choose their own path. All we could do is educate them, try to bring understanding, and leave it to them. We saw, after a while, that the influences of other races coming in, trading… etc., it was too tempting. And so, there was an ascension of those who chose to not stay and regress into the full amnesia. We went into the bliss of our light bodies.

[This] of course, [is the] time that you are in now.

The descendants who remained lived for a time with the original values and then moved on into further and further forgetting, competition and conquering, until indeed they were conquered.

And all the cities were abandoned and the sickness from the West and the East all flooded in and the people began to die.

This is a very common scene, when you consider when a people become so far from their original instructions… their own consciousness will create a catalyst for death and rebirth.

DUANE: So, prior to that sickness, is it fair to say that you mortally lived very, very, very long lives?

ASCENDED BEINGS OF KOHUNLICH: Oh yes, indeed.

DUANE: It feels like, if we could go back to that time before the forgetting and the sickness we would probably see you as gods. Is that true?

Or just people living their lives?

ASCENDED BEINGS OF KOHUNLICH: You are the descendants of very many races. You are more intelligent even than we were.

We may have been carrying the wisdom of our ancestors as close as we could... We may have been meditating with our star ancestors and helpers...We knew to subscribe to love, so at that time we could be [likened to] your siblings. We of course had more advanced perception, as our organs of perception, [pineal glands] were still much larger than yours are now, yet, you [are] much further along through the forgetting times and at the birthing of the next golden epoch, yes? This makes you strong with all the wisdom of having journeyed through the darkness within you.

You have died.

You have disintegrated.

You have experienced, as a species, everything that you are not, to birth into your pure essence of who you are. Therefore, we are able to communicate with you because of this. And... when you ascend you will be carrying all of this wisdom with you and leaping further than we leapt when we ascended. You see? It was our time to ascend… that we can be where we are now to assist you. That was our choice. Our journey to do. Your journey is different. No ascension journey is the same. Everyone and every group and every community and every race has its own journey as an aspect of the divine…Each is so diverse.

We have great sympathy/compassion for you because we also lived in the time of the death… The death of what we knew. You [experience this] from the other side of [the epoch], the opposite side [from us]. Yet, there is still a very strong grieving when what you have known begins to fall away and dismantle.

We look into you now and see where you hold your grief and fear, yet, we also look into you and transmit our joy to you… And we would say there is so much more to be joyful for.

DUANE: Yes!

ASCENDED BEINGS OF KOHUNLICH: This is indeed a time of celebration. Continue to unplug from all of the holograms that would cloud your vision. You see, the dark times have passed, they're done! The hologram wants people to believe they're not. So, they continue to weave stronger and stronger illusions. But the people are free now in the light. So, give thanks to the underworld for all you've learned, but the seed is reaching...has broken the surface and is reaching for the Sun. And it is your work to point people to the light streaming from the Sun, the transmission from the Sun. This is the sustenance the people need now. They have the soil, the minerals, the water...They know the underworld...Their roots are deep through all the experiences had...

Now it is time for the Sun.

You must let go and surrender yourself to the Sun.

Lift the people up!

(Pause)

It is a pleasure to be sharing this moment with you.

(Pause)

There is a way that humanity, you, seekers, fear the hologram, fear the illusions being woven...

And THAT is being in the illusion.

The illusion wants you to be afraid that it is more powerful than you, that it can control you and manipulate you. It wants you to be paranoid that you are never free of it...Even when you have a moment of freedom, you then doubt, [and consider] that you are not actually free of it, "Maybe this is still the illusion..." This is the trick.

Let go, relax, breath and feel the pleasure of breath, the sounds of nature...The pleasure of being... Just sitting and connecting with your love, the Universe within you...

THIS IS REAL.

When you close your eyes and go within and expand into the infinity that you are...This is Real...and that is where the Sun is.

The Sun is at your core...

The Sun of your own awakened consciousness...

This is your home.

And so, you are supporting people to unplug from the external obsessions, looking outside themselves constantly. Help people turn their gaze inward and feel the light of their own radiant essence.

(End of Transmission)

Are you having a moment of deeper insight into how history repeats itself right now? Wow! I am most struck by the part where they say, "This is a very common scene, when you consider when a people become so far from their original instructions... their own [collective] consciousness will create a catalyst for death and rebirth." This is such a powerful invitation to understand more deeply how we played a part in the creation of our current upheavals. I know I was praying for years for sanity, honesty, freedom, and peace. I do believe that the collective desire for a new, healthy civilization on Earth generated a catalyst to launch us into it. More of us desired to wake up, than to stay asleep. More of use desired to be free, than to stay enslaved. Yet, I also believe that at this juncture, we can choose to not repeat history again. This can be the end of cycling through this pain. At the close of this grand cycle, we can choose love over fear, service-to-others over service-to-self, and move on into higher octaves.

One last paragraph to pay homage to the ascended Giants of Kohunlich:

The revered ascended giants we met in Kohunlich, I believe, were some of the original races on our planet. Giants who used to walk the Earth whose ancestors before them came from off-planet and inhabited this Earth for thousands, perhaps tens of thousands of years. Then, they just disappeared? But we have proof of their presence in their bones left in tombs, sarcophaguses, and beneath the ground. When did they depart from our Earth? In how many waves and over how many generations? Perhaps at the time of the great flood? These ascended ones from Kohunlich, and others like them whom we've connected with from many sacred sites around world, all were linked to nature, crystals, animals, water, and especially the Sun, in a loving, intimate and ecstatic way. They were spiritually awake and full of timeless wisdom, giving them access to what I want to call Universal libraries of information. They were galactic and dimensional travelers, yet still so caring for all life on the Earth. I continue to be deeply moved and honored by every encounter I have with them.

CHAPTER 15

SOLAR ACTIVITY AND ASCENSION

In the Ra transmissions, it's explained that 75,000 Earth years is one grand cycle or octave for third density. Yet, if the planet does not expand in consciousness to the degree needed for ascension, another grand cycle will begin, rather than moving on into fourth density. There are three smaller cycles within one grand cycle, of 25,000 years each. Each 25,000-year cycle is an opportunity for souls to ascend into higher density. Ra explains that the timing of Harvest, as they call it, or ascension, is like clockwork and arrives inevitably on time. Now we are at one of those opportunities for Harvest or Ascension again, at the tail end of a grand cycle of 75,000 years.

Apart from the Law of One information, I have been researching our Sun's innate cycles of renewal. Approximately every 25,000 years, as it is documented by both Zoroastrian and Hindu ancient writings as well as descriptions appearing in other cultures, our Sun goes through a full coronal discharge that engulfs any planets orbiting closest to it. In ancient Vedic texts this is called the Samvartaka Fire. Now recall the July 24, 2012 CME's (Coronal Mass Ejection) that almost hit Earth. This is when the sun expels her whole coronal mass, not just a solar flare. It's a huge deal! Could an even larger discharge be coming in the future?

From Wikipedia:

> In this story, samvartaka is depicted as a raging fire. In the works of Garga, an influential Vedic sage in ancient India, samvartaka is described as a devastating, energetic force that will arrive as one of two comets. In the sage's words, "Like the stellar wheel rotating (repeating) in the sky, the comet-wheel also repeats in the sky.
>
> In Hinduism and Jainism, Sāmvartaka is a divine force or power normally used by the deity Indra. Described as being a cloud of energy or fire, the force is used to destroy or despoil that which displeases Indra. The force is referenced to in Hindu and Jainist texts.[22]

Ra doesn't refer to a time of solar emissions, but does speak to major climactic upheaval when a planet transitions from one density to the next.

The solar event, when it happens, will elicit a state of bliss or ecstatic communion with the Divine for those who

---

[22] https://en.wikipedia.org/wiki/S%C4%81%E1%B9%81vartaka. Accessed on April 28, 2020 on Wikipedia.

have been doing their inner-work. Yet, for those who have resisted change and growth, and have been choosing denial or wounded consciousness, this solar event could be extremely frightening and, at worst, induce a psychotic break.

Here is an excerpt from an insightful article by Dr. Schavi M. Ali, published in Disclosure News Italia on April 28, 2020:

Major Cosmic Cleansing On The Horizon!

By Dr. Schavi M. Ali

It has been reported by science institutes around the globe that just south of our Sun's equator, a sunspot is growing which could result in a solar flare exploding with photons, electrons, carbon dioxide gases, etc. which would activate a powerful cleansing energy on Earth/Gaia.

This would possibly begin initially in the Pacific Rim, but its energetics would affect the entire planet.

Spiritually, this cosmic occurrence is for purposes of clearing-out ancient space/time continuums (time lines) in which were experiences of hatreds and warfare and subsequent damages to the Nature upon Earth/Gaia which spun the planet into many eons of further disharmony which has now eventuated into the tremendously traumatic conditions of depletion of the vitality of water, soil, air, people, animals, plants, etc.

In other words, the "Kali Yuga" ("Age of Chaos") has been raging on the planet for many thousands of years. Earth/Gaia has reached a point whereby a deeper cleansing, other than those which have already been occurring for many years, must now happen.

"Sattva Yuga" ("Age of Peace") must be born! The collective consciousness of humanity has certainly increased in recent decades; however, there are still many who do not understand the "Higher Laws" of SOURCE, and accordingly, they are yet steeped in political, sociological, and philosophical turmoil which affects their physiology, mental states, and emotional responses. "Lightbringers" (often also called "Lightworkers") — Teachers of Higher Laws, Energy Healers, Spiritual Gurus, etc. — are doing their utmost to assist in the elevation of consciousness of those who lack knowledge and also in the support of those who are already quite elevated in understanding. The collective Vibrational Frequency of reception and transmission of such individuals soars into the ethereal realms where spiritual atomic and sub-atomic particles act as receivers and transmitters, and when cosmic forces are in reception of messages from any planet or *galaxy, their ethereal consciousness formulates a plan to help the planet or galaxy which is calling for help and guidance.*

All solar flares can create activations in the Chakra Systems of humanity, and obviously, the stronger the flaring is, the more pronounced are the activations... Remember, Earth/Gaia and all creation upon "Her" are in the labor of re-birth. The building-up of solar flares, which may be released from our Sun any time soon, is likened to "spiritual forceps" which bring forth new time lines.[23]

In a channeling session on July 27, 2019, in response to Duane asking a question about this solar event and if it's real or is really going to happen, the Higher Density Helpers transmitted this answer through me:

---

[23] https://www.disclosurenews.it/en/major-cosmic-cleansing-on-the-horizon/. Dr. Schavi M. Ali article I found in Disclosure New Italia. Accessed on April 28, 2020.

Our Solar Star's Ascension Moment

July 27, 2019

We will speak to the astrological, geological and solar spiritual cycles of your current timeline. Every planet moves through geological shifting and transformation. The planet you know as Venus, even now is evolving into her next form. Once she was a lush and populated planet like Earth is now. In your mind you might say she has digressed, yet this would be untrue.

The planets of your solar system, you could say they are the children of your great solar star. The Sun feeds your planet nourishment, like a Mother tending to young. All of the planets in your solar star's magnetic field are impacted greatly by the consciousness of your solar star. The solar star, your Sun, is a living consciousness. It is a being. It is a God Presence, who, just like you, is evolving and becoming more and more aware of Self and moving into higher and higher densities. It is a Creator God, yes, but you must understand the infinite nature of becoming. The solar star that is your Sun is becoming her next emanation.

You could say that she wants to take a deep inhale and stretch into her next vast awareness and size and presence. In doing so, she throws off solar flares and emissions of plasma. And as her body is thrown into the atmospheres of her children, the planets, they receive her light. They receive the transmission of her evolutionary ecstatic experience into their ionospheres. The planets closest to her body will receive the strongest transmission and therefore the strongest opportunity to upgrade with her.

Yet, all of the bodies within her field will transform because they are a part of her. As she awakens to the next experience of herself, she will purify the bodies of her children like a lioness cleaning her cubs. She will purify and cleanse the planets that they may leap with her into this new octave.

Those who are attuned to her, those who are attuned to this Creator presence and the infinite Source within themselves; those who understand that when you connect to the great Sun that you are; then you match and entrain to her God consciousness. This is an ecstatic opening for you. It is desired. It is natural. It is joyful.

For the ones upon your planet who have woven webs of lies to entrap and domesticate a slave force... for those who have found that living within the delusion has given them power and they are comfortable in it; those who are choosing to stay in the What They're Not, they will not experience this as ecstasy. They will experience this as incineration.

They will experience it as suffering. There are many who will leave their physical forms to escape the suffering. They will continue to cycle through the negative polarity as long as they need to, to achieve their great awakening into the positive polarity and the ecstatic reunion, at last.

(End of Transmission)

What I understand from this transmission is that our Sun will undergo her own changing – her heat, light and radiation output will be elevating. Those who ascend with her will feel this simultaneous with their own opening and expansion, thus it will be blissful. Those who stay in 3D, will experience just the physicality of it – the intensity of the heat, the blinding light and more radiation entering Earth's atmosphere.

Here is a quote from Ra on the physical and metaphysical ascension journey of our Sun:

> In relationship to the densities, the sun body may physically, as you would say, be seen to be a large body of gaseous elements undergoing the processes of fusion and radiating heat and light.

> Metaphysically, the sun achieves a meaning to fourth through seventh density according to the growing abilities of entities in these densities to grasp the living creation and co-entity, or other-self, nature of

this sun body. Thus, by the sixth density the sun may be visited and inhabited by those dwelling in time/space and may even be partially created from moment to moment by the processes of sixth-density entities in their evolution.[24]

My translation of this is: As third density humanity becomes more self-aware and unconditionally loving, we awaken to the consciousness of the vaster bodies we are a part of. The Sun is a Creator presence of our solar system. To recognize this and open to commune to this consciousness can accelerate both the individual's ascension and the Sun's ascension. By the time we reach sixth density, we (as light bodies) will be able to enter into the solar Creator light bodies. One may even choose to reside within the love-light realm of this aspect of Intelligent Infinity. When the Higher Dimensional Helpers speak to Duane and I of the Council of the Sun, they are reminding us that our true natures are sixth to seventh density, and we are from the Infinite God Realms of Love-Light, accessed through communion with our Sun.

Remember, in 1981 Ra told the L/L Research team that there were 65 million Wanderers incarnate on Earth, and most of these are sixth density beings. Many people of these

---

[24] https://www.lawofone.info/results.php?q=the+sun+body. From transcription 41.4. Accessed on April 27, 2021.

sixth density Wanderers on the planet right now are Council of the Sun representatives here to assist in Planetary Ascension. The Helpers have told us there are Council of the Sun representatives on every planet in our solar system, stationed there to help guide planetary energies towards ascension. This isn't just about Earth. This is about our solar system! It's a family affair!

Some believe a major solar event is coming, within 8 to 50 years, that will complete this "octave" of Earth, and begin a new Golden Age.

Our Galaxy Will Catalyze Our Sun

Let's explore more evidence of these ascension times...

NASA has discovered a concentration of photons in the arm of our galaxy where Earth's solar system is located. NASA has been calling it "Local or Cosmic Fluff." Some say that, as this concentration of light and ionically charged particles hits our heliosphere (Sun's orbit), they will activate Solar activity and put pressure on our planet's protective field. This will impact human consciousness and biology. It will accelerate transformation! NASA reports that we are well into the middle of this local cosmic cloud right now that measures 30 light-years wide.

The Maya refer to the Cosmic Fluff as the Photon Belt, and describe it as a space/time distortion that catalyzes and expands consciousness. The photon belt encircles and goes through the Pleiadian Constellation, whose brightest star (as seen from Earth), Alcyone, is acknowledge to be our Great Central Sun. In their ancient codices, the Maya recorded how our solar system satellites around The Pleiades, as do all the celestial bodies at a certain distance out from these Seven Sisters. Wow! Why aren't we taught this in school? The passage of our solar system through the photon belt is said to last for 2000 years. [25]

On January 9, 2020, Duane and I did a channeling session in which we asked the Higher Density Helpers what we could expect in 2020, as far as catalysts are concerned. This is how the Arcturian Council responded:

2020 CATALYSTS FOR HARVEST TIME

January 9, 2021

DUANE: Can you talk more about the catalysts we can expect in 2020?

---

[25] Information on the Mayan Wisdom Teachings can found at CasaKin.org, Miguel Angel founder. https://casakin.org/foundational-teachings/

ARCTURIAN COUNCIL: We will introduce ourselves. We are the an Arcturian collective who watches over your planet and engages with humanity as counselors during this time of evolution for your species.

Your year, 2020, which is a misnomer, as it is not truly an accurate numerological identification of linear time of your planet, nor of humanity's existence on your planet. It is simply the designed calendar enforced upon your planet by the Illuminati, as you say, at the beginning of the power-over paradigm that moved specifically through religious organizations.

Yet for simplicities sake, we will use this terminology. The next 365 days, less now, that you are on the ninth day, does include many planetary alignments that produce such magnetic qualities, that there is an enhanced polarity shift within humanity's consciousness. There is a pull to make a choice towards love or fear.

There will be external circumstances that will act as catalyst, so that the internal pressure to make a choice will be mirrored and matched by an external pressure as well.

The theme of course, of 2020 we would say— given what we've observed of the desires of the heart-field across your planet, the desires of the heart-field of humanity— is generating a movement for what has been hidden to come into the Light. This is enacted as well within each person as desire to see what is hidden within yourselves and bring it into the light. These two go together. There are contingencies of negative polarity consciousness upon the planet that have been manipulating the masses, and the people have been in denial, avoidance, or rejection of knowing the truth about this, though it's in their face every single day. And now the dreaming of the masses is to know the truth. This speaks to a grand awakening does it not? To NOT want to know, and now, to want to KNOW. You are certainly in the quickening of the momentum of awakening now. You will perhaps notice that there is not just awakening in humanity, but also in the animals of higher consciousness. The felines, canines, horses, the apes, the elephants... These ones as well will be ascending into higher consciousness with you. You may find more accessible telepathic communication with these beings on the planet now.

Humanity is going through a portal of purification and cleansing—one of the final portals before ascension into fourth dimension.

Collective humanity shares a great communal neural network and it is now rewiring and becoming a new neural network. For you must realize that the billions of you human beings on the planet have such an impact upon what happens in the reality sphere you're in. You cannot go through such a massive awakening process without the external world mirroring it back to you, as the external world is the hologram of your consciousness.

The fires are your anger. The ferocity of learning the truth and being enraged by it. Through the catalyst of feeling powerless, you learn deeper levels of surrender from which greater empowerment comes.

The flooding and mudslides are your collective grief. When you learn the truth and are heart broken by it. Through this catalyst you learn renewal and resiliency from deeper emotional vulnerability and honesty.

Hurricanes and tornadoes are the mental anguish and confusion once the truth is learned, yet through this catalyst comes the energy for problem solving and taking action to build new more intelligent structures.

Earthquakes come from the strength of truth shaking untruths out of the fabric of society. The denials are made known. The light shines on the shame hidden deep in the crevices within you. What was in the depths rises to the surface. Now these parts of you can be seen, loved, and integrated into the whole.

(End of Transmission)

NASA satellite footage and images captured of the other planets in our solar system show that "Climate Change" is not exclusive to the Earth. Mars, Venus, Neptune, Saturn, Jupiter are all showing climate changes as well. Lakes of water are appearing at the poles of Mars, for example. This is a very challenging fact for people to look at, because this being true makes the stories fed to people about global warming and climate change then false. Namely, that humanity is the cause of global warming, we are guilty, and now we must make huge sacrifices to "atone for our sins".

When people find out the truth about our Sun and Ascension, they will realize all of this was inevitable. The volcanic activity, earthquakes, ice caps melting, etc. The Photon Belt, which our solar system is traveling through now, will catalyze transformation on all levels. This is our entry into an age of peace, prosperity, creativity and higher consciousness. As I noted earlier, Ra tells us that it is our own confusion about who we are and the choice we face now that is causing a more dramatic transition into 4th Density. If we were told the truth... if we had not been enslaved... if we had had access to our true heritage...the transition would be smoother.

CHAPTER 16

TWO EARTHS?

The concept of two Earths has been around for decades. In 2011 the movie "Another Earth" was one of the winners at the Sundance Film Festival. In the film, original Earth's astronomers receive signals and then visuals of a mirror image of Earth in the sky. It turns out to be a parallel timeline Earth, where another you existed and maybe made different choices. An invitation went out for a small number of people to have the opportunity to meet themselves on the other Earth.

In 2016 NASA scientists and researchers of Cosmic Rays in Antarctica discovered something unexpected. An article was written in the New Scientist interviewing the program director in April of 2020 entitled, *We May Have Found a Parallel Universe Going Backward in Time.*[26] The article states: "That strange finding was made in 2016.

---

[26] https://www.newscientist.com/article/2229988-strange-particles-found-in-antarctica-cannot-be-explained-by-physics/ Accessed on December 10, 2021.

Since then, all sorts of suggestions rooted in known physics have been put forward to account for the perplexing signal, and all have been ruled out. What's left is shocking in its implications. Explaining this signal requires the existence of a topsy-turvy universe created in the same big bang as our own and existing in parallel with it. In this mirror world, positive is negative, left is right and time runs backwards.

Even though I pull from NASA information in this book, I actually am quite skeptical of what they offer to the public. I believe that there is a mix of truth and lies on their website. They are another authority figure in the matrix designed to keep us blocked from our true history. That's why Duane and I prefer to hold our sessions with the Higher Dimensional Helpers, who we've come to love and trust.

Here's a channeling from March 28, 2021, which was the full moon in Libra, where Grand Master Qi, a Higher Dimensional Helper from the Dragon Council, replied to a question from Duane on the topic of two Earths:

TWO EARTHS?

March 28, 2021

DUANE: Will we physically see a separation between third density and fourth density Earths? Will there become two earth-like planets? And those choosing the higher density will be on one and those choosing to stay in 3D will be on another. Is that a true statement or is that not true?

GRAND MASTER QI: This question comes from a third density perspective. (Laughter) That there will be two similar density physical earths and they will look like each other? No. You see, there are already many, many higher dimensional planes of existence and many, many civilizations who have ascended and are on higher planes, yet they may be the same location. Like for example, your Mt. Shasta area. For example, this island that you live on. And many other places of your third density planet have ascended already and there are already beings living in these fourth, fifth, and higher density realms of these earthly locations. It does look very different in the higher realms.

In the higher densities, we would say between the higher fourth, going into fifth, there is a very different perception of reality. And the structures are much more vibrational. The fifth density and higher are realms that can be entered into and visited just through directing your thought and you are there.

It is not that fifth density Souls, who have incarnated into third density bodies on a third density planet, that they can disappear from one physical location and suddenly appear in another physical location, no. Upon their choice to incarnate into third density to serve, they are subject to the split consciousness of the density, yet have access to their higher density information. They are subject to the laws of nature in the third density. Only in a light body in the higher dimensions can beings phase in and out, including to visit a lower density realm. A third density physical body cannot phase in and out like this just from making a decision to do so, because you are in a linear time consciousness. But a light body, attuned to nonlinear time/space, can do this.

And so, you see it is an ascension process. It is the literal transmutation of flesh. The energy of your Soul and the essence of your physicality – DNA - creates for yourself a higher dimensional form that exists in the higher dimensions.

You have had experiences already where the higher dimensional beings phase into your reality and give you a glimpse... perhaps you see a burst of light, an orb, or a light being suddenly appear and disappear. That's us.

And when you take on your light body again, you will be able to phase in and out of 3D like this as well. You can visit for a moment, and then phase out, but you never leave your home dimension, unless you choose to live fully in a third dimensional body on a third dimensional planet, do you see?

And so, in simple terms we can answer your question and say, oh yes, there are countless Earths...

DUANE: Got it. They're all in the same place. Just in different dimensions. Different densities.

In corroboration of this channeled information, I found this quote one month later in the Law of One, Ra Material, on the Scorpio full moon.

Here's what Ra says on this same topic:

Ra: You must see the Earth, as you call it, as being seven Earths. There is red, orange, yellow, and there will soon be a completed green color vibratory locus for fourth-density entities which they will call Earth. During the fourth-density experience, due to the lack of development of fourth-density entities, the third-density planetary sphere is not useful for habitation since the early fourth-density entity will not know precisely how to maintain the illusion that fourth density cannot be seen or determined from any instrumentation available to any third density.

Thus, in fourth density the red, orange, and green energy nexi of your planet will be activated while the yellow is in potentiation along with the blue and the indigo.

May we ask at this time if there be any brief queries?

Questioner: OK. Now as this transition continues into fourth-density activation, in order to inhabit this fourth-density sphere it will be necessary for all third-density physical bodies to go through the process which we refer to as death. Is this correct?

Ra: I am Ra. This is correct. [27]

Given this information, we are taught from the Higher Helpers that there *are* multiple Earth's right now, yet existing at different dimensional levels. There is a correlation between the maturity of our consciousness and the dimensional Earth we live on and are able to perceive. As we ascend, we phase into higher realms of reality.

Duane and I perceive a higher dimensional Hawaii. We see rainbows in the sunsets every night. We see orbs, plasma ships (colored energy UFOs), and ancient Lemurians coming through into this realm to teach us. Most people on the island aren't perceiving these things and would likely be skeptical if we told them about it. How can two totally different realities exist in the same place? We also noticed this during the 2020 lock-downs. 2020 ended up being a very lucrative year for Duane's business. He coached his employees to stay positive, loving and "down-to-earth"

---

[27] https://www.lawofone.info/results.php?q=seven+earths. Transcription 62.29. Accessed on April 26, 2021.

with their customers. They envisioned prosperity with ease through the lock-downs, and that's exactly what happened for them. Duane has been committed to ushering his business into 4th Density in the positive polarity. "Keep Choosing Love", he tells his team. Yet, many people in our lives went the other way. They felt terrified of getting sick, and were afraid to touch people. The isolation brought on waves of depression and even despair from the lack of sunlight and physical touch. Many also faced severe financial break down and insecurity.

The Higher Dimensional Helpers and Ra Collective also share with us that we must leave our denser physical bodies behind to ascend into a higher dimensional Earth. Remember that each density is an octave. And within each octave are sub-octaves. So, we are ascending CONSTANTLY! We are evolving through seven levels of consciousness within our current 3rd Density, and when we get to the eighth sub-octave, this is also the first step of 4th Density. This is the TRANSITION PHASE.

There comes a point when we do need to transmute the flesh of our lower-density body, but until then, our current bodies will be the vehicles through which we serve during this amazing transition. Yet, remember! We are entering into a Golden Age right now and being human is not going to feel like what it used to in the inverted matrix! Soon we will be able to enjoy amazing advanced technologies previously hidden from the public, coming out! Such as "Med Beds", or what the Arcturian Medical

Guild calls "Holographic Chambers or Pods". With a healthy and whole current Body-Mind-Spirit, experiencing the transitional phase between 3rd and 4th densities will be an adventure!

CHAPTER 17

ASCENSION AND THE ASTRAL PLANET

Part of the split in consciousness in Third Density is between waking life and our dreamtime. Yet, as discussed earlier, when we are in our astral bodies we can be predated upon by 4th dimensional negative entities. One of my energy medicine teachers when I was 22 once said to me, "Being truly awake means you are equally conscious during the day and during your astral travels." She was promoting having an energy hygiene practice for our Astral Bodies. I'll share some of these later in this section.

Reclaiming your fragments is an ongoing commitment. One innate measuring device you have to gauge how you're doing is your dreams! Your dreams can direct you to part of yourself that is still frozen in traumatic memories, stories, behaviors or habits. They can also show you where you are being diverted, blocked or entrapped in the reversal grids.

In 2017 Duane and I traveled to Beijing, China on business. We stayed in a four-star hotel in the Western district where everything feels like the United States. Beneath the ground floor of our hotel was a massive underground shopping mall, four stories deep. I woke up one morning from a dream that I was in that underground mall, wandering in circles, trying to find my way to natural light. The mall truly was set up to confuse, like a maze. I realized in that moment that the design was purposeful. Guests staying at the hotel from out of the city and, more likely, out of the country, were subject to this architecture of confusion, and the result was entrapment of the Astral Body. There was no way you could stray beyond that loci and explore what was happening in the real China.

What is the Astral Body?

The astral body is our light-body. Some say it appears as a mirror image of you, but etheric. Ra refers to the Astral Body as the Ka, or the Indigo-ray Body. This is how our consciousness travels when our physical bodies are asleep. It is connected through magnetic charge to our physical form until our death. At that point, this magnetism "switches off," to put it simply, and our Souls are released from attachment to physicality.

The Astral body is free from the limitations of the physical body. When in dreamtime, we can take on any shape or form, go anywhere in ordinary or non-ordinary reality instantaneously and we can travel anywhere within or outside of our current timeline. I once had a dream where I lived 50 years of a woman's life in what was probably just one-hour.

Remember the split? Well, waking consciousness is one half of that and the astral awareness is the other half. When awake, most of us rarely remember what we did for hours and hours on the astral planes. When we're asleep, we don't continue our to-do list of waking consciousness, we are in a whole new situation/environment/family/land/planet... Yet, we can bridge this divide. We can begin to remember more of our dreams and we can become lucid while in our dreaming.

Dreaming 'At Cause'

In the longer Light Leader programs I offer, I invite my students to practice "Being at Cause." When we live our lives At Cause, we are choosing to be awake and intentional on our path. We are steering the vessel of our lives, rather than sitting in the backseat feeling out of control, ambivalent or defeated. We are calling the shots, commanding what we want, and taking actions towards making things happen. Oppositely, and more commonly, people live 'at effect,' as victims to their reality. Things are happening 'to' or 'at' them. They feel out of control of what might happen next and often brace themselves for what may be coming around the bend.

The exercise I give my students is to 'Wake Up at Cause' in the morning. To start your day with intention, prayer, and gratitude is very empowering! When I first learned this practice in my mid-twenties, I would wake up and get very specific: "I want to have a big belly laugh with someone today. I want to miss all traffic. I want to find a new, inspiring book to read." And you know, everything I requested would always happen. I wouldn't realize it until later, after the belly laughs and the new book was in my hand, I'd suddenly remember, "Oh my God! I manifested this!" Waking Up at Cause is a major shift for most people, because most of us experience waking up as going right into unconscious, habitual behavior. "I didn't get enough sleep," was my common refrain. Going right into the to-do list or taking care of others needs before you've even had a glass of water... These choices start one's day off 'at effect'.

Once my students get used to waking up 'at cause' and feeling the benefit of that, I ask them to begin a practice of going to sleep 'at cause'. This supports the sovereignty of the Astral Body while traveling at night.

Here's how this works:

1.   Once in bed, before falling asleep, make the affirmation that your Astral Body is surrounded in your Eternal Soul Light and protected by All that is Good in the Universe.

2.   Affirm that your physical body is in a bubble of protective Eternal Soul Light, as well, and refresh your grounding connection to Mother Earth for your body.

3.   Affirm that the 'silver cord'[28], that connects your Astral Body to your Physical Body, is also refreshed and in present time and protected.

4.   Speak out loud: "I affirm that my Astral Body will depart from my solar plexus, not the top of my head, to travel tonight. I affirm that all doors of deception, false time-lines, reverse grids, illusion and trauma are closed. I affirm all doors of love, truth, the harmonic eternal time-line of Earth/Gaia, are open."

5.   At this point, I might speak my intention for my astral travels: "I am going to the celestial ocean to commune with the whales," or "I would like to

---

[28] The Silver Cord is referred to in many metaphysical texts recording the experiences of people who have astral projected and seen a silvery thread connecting their light body to their sleeping or meditating physical body. The silver cord has been experienced as connecting the pineal glands of both bodies, or with some people as connecting the solar plexus of both bodies. Its function is to transfer the information received during astral travel to the physical body so it can be applied to waking life. At mortal death, the silver cord is dissolved and the light body is released into the spiritual realms.

receive a healing tonight." Whatever makes you happy!

6.   Finally, I affirm I will remember all pertinent information upon waking up in the morning, and my astral body will enter back into my physical body through my solar plexus with no interference.

Back to Beijing

So, I woke up that morning realizing that the architecture was a purposeful design. That entrapping the Astral Body was a thing... That negative polarity beings will endeavor to trap the astral consciousness of people during dreamtime to keep them in the matrix/reverse grids, where they can feed off of them. They don't want us to wake up, because if we remember we are eternal, we can't be controlled anymore.

Our astral body expresses our eternal nature and reminds us of the higher abilities we have, even in Third Density. Have you ever experienced telepathy, levitation, or flying in a dream? Astral travel has long been developed in secret militaries around the world for "black ops" and espionage. It is a skill that can be used as a weapon, or as a gift to humanity. Imagine if regular people started developing their astral body abilities and couldn't be trapped anymore?

One way that they've been entrapping our astral bodies is through the proliferation of violent material in our movies, shows, video games, and other so-called entertainment. Most people engage with this material at night before bed and don't consider to clear their energy bodies before sleep. This allows for the violent material to create blocks to astral body empowerment. The negative imagery and messages infiltrate the dream state and can begin to not only control one's astral plane experiences but also rewire your physiology for heightened paranoia, addiction, phobias and insecurity.

One anonymous Yogi said this: "A fear that captures our whole attention generates the repetition of negative images and affirmations. It holds within it the power to materialize itself into reality." Our waking and dreaming lives are intricately interwoven and greatly impact each other! Your body needs nourishing, vital food to thrive, right? Your astral body needs nourishing food too. As Grand Master Qi once taught us: "Events and experiences that happen during your day will be processed and metabolized by your nighttime self. Whatever your nighttime-self experiences will be processed and integrated by your daytime-self. One paves the way for the other, so there is always growth. That is how you are designed".

What happens when we continuously compile trauma into our system with no clearing or healing? We will develop recurring nightmares and discordant dreams. This is an astral body illness. Yet, every repetitive dream is also an opportunity for our astral body to wake us up. If we can become lucid in the repetitive dream, realize what the message is and shift our lives accordingly, we've broken the cycle! I will talk about how to do this in the next section.

After the horrible entrapment dream in the underground mall in Beijing, I shifted my frequency each of the following nights through prayer, high-frequency music and energetic set up, and never astral traveled into the mall again. In fact, my dreams shifted positively, yet the Higher Dimensional Helpers kept repeating to take extra precaution and do mindful energetic set up daily and nightly. Beijing was the most psychically dangerous place I'd ever visited.

Soul Retrieval & Dream Work

Until you become adept at lucid dreaming, you can do Soul Retrieval work when you're awake. Soul Retrieval is a process of rescuing your Soul fragments from frozen states, as described earlier. The best time to do this is right when you wake up. Stay in the position you were in when you had the dream. This tends to invoke the memory of it right back into your consciousness. In a relaxed state go back into the dream to the moment of discomfort. Request your Higher Self to show you what the dream is unveiling. Then, invite your dream self to leave the repetitive dream environment and come home with you. I will often infuse the dream environment with spiritual fire and harmonic sounds, breaking it apart into particles of light. I will then plant a seed of truth into the fertile soil of my dreamtime. I close the Soul Retrieval with integrating my dream-self back into my physical body with me. I bath her in a shower of loving-light and tell her she is now free. I ask her what brings her joy, and envision her empowered, joyful and whole.

Medicine Dreams

Now I want to talk about the opposite side of the spectrum of the dream world: Medicine Dreams! I believe that when we receive a very lucid, vivid, and magical dream, there is a major message breaking through the hologram from the eternal realms to support us. Medicine Dreams often carry a higher spiritual feeling to them, such as an animal appears to you but they are giant and radiating light. Or an Ancestor visits but they look young and vibrant and have a serenity exuding from them. Medicine Dreams seem to always make sure you wake up in a way to remember them – you hear your name being called, your cat jumps on you, or an event in the dream will jolt you awake. Often, when we recall one of these dreams, it will flood back in detail, as if we'd just had it last night. These powerful dream events are wake up calls at important moments on your timeline... Moments when you face a fork in the road. You can either step further onto the path of spiritual initiation, or further away from it.

Some people are born with a special gift of dreaming, which I call "Dream Medicine". People with dream medicine will tend to have dreams to guide the collective, not just themselves. Many people in my family carry dream medicine, including me. In 2017, I had a dream that showed me the transformation that was coming to our planet. I named this dream, "Fall of the Oligarchs". Here it is:

FALL OF THE OLIGARCHS

I am with my mother, grandmother, and my friend Liz, and a young pregnant couple. It is daylight going into dusk. We are in a city that looks like it has been bombed to rubble. Buildings are toppled. The place is deserted.

In a town square type of area there is a statue still standing of a military official who had also been the president or leader of the country. He is bald and feels like Stalin or Mao or someone like that.

Suddenly there is an earthquake. We all catch ourselves from falling. Then the head of the statue cracks and falls off. It rolls on the ground by my feet. Then the whole statue starts crumbling as the earthquake gets stronger. We realize this is the moment of apocalypse or the end-times.

There is a hill of grassy-green just outside of town. On top of the hill is a white gazebo. We all look at each other and decide we'll split up and make a run for the hilltop. We know that the hilltop is the ultimate destination. If we can make it, then we'll have survived the collapse of civilization.

I go with my grandmother. She leads. We run past the crumbling statue and, with the ground shaking beneath our feet, we run up a dirt hill that leads to the hilltop. As we run, something zips past me almost tripping me up. I realize it was a shard from the statue. The pieces of statue are still alive with the menace of that old paradigm. They are shooting over the ground at us, ankle high, as if shot from machine guns, trying to take us down. My grandmother is quick on her feet, nimbly hopping over the shards before they trip her. I stay focused and manage to not fall.

We make it to the top of the hill and, with relief, enter the gazebo panting. At the same time, my mother, friend, and the couple enter from other pathways. The couple has had their baby and the woman holds the infant in her arms.

The earthquake has stopped. We realize it's sunrise and we all face the east. The sun rises and golden rays stream across the landscape into our faces. We are jubilant, feeling triumphant and relieved. We know the new age has just begun.

I knew when I woke that this dream was not for me alone; that it was prophetic. Later that year I had an opportunity to describe the dream to an audience of people at a conference on Shamanism. My dream was collected into a compilation of "medicine dreams for the masses" by a dream researcher. That my dream was able to serve others felt deeply meaningful to me.

If you have had prophetic dreams, please share them. Create a video, write a blog, but get the messages of the eternal realms out there for people to benefit from. They aren't called medicine dreams for nothing. The medicine we carry is to be shared with our communities. If we hoard or hide our 'medicine,' we will experience Soul loss.

Here is another very powerful dream that came through in 2018, clearly preparing us for ascension:

5D EARTH EXISTS NOW

I am in my childhood home. It is daytime. There is a commotion outside in the cul-de-sac. I go down the stairs into the living room from my bedroom. There are people in my house, wandering around. They don't look right. Something's off. I open the front door and look out. Charcoal grey spheres a little larger than softballs are flying over the neighborhood. They are like drones. Each one stops at a designated point, forming a grid through the neighborhood. The spheres descend to about 10 feet above the ground. A red light is blinking in a center band on each sphere.

I walk out the front door and into my driveway. I feel afraid. The spheres seem to be some kind of martial law, social control device. Just then, several silver three-sided pyramids drop from the sky. Or maybe they just appear. They are shiny and reflecting the blue sky. There is one just three feet from me.

Suddenly my friend Diane appears. She is a friend who passed away from cancer in 2016. She comes to me smiling and says, "Look!", pointing to the pyramid. I walked to the closest pyramid and it responds to me by growing to my height, with the base touching the ground. The face opens like a sliding door. I look through the portal and to my surprise I'm looking down onto San Francisco Bay Area from above. I see the Marina, Presidio, Golden Gate Bridge and Sausalito. Everything looks different − vibrant, harmonic, flowing. I focus in on the Presidio. The structures are in harmony with nature. There are no more freeways. People are traveling without combustion engine vehicles over the land and sea. The air is clean. The water's sparkling.

My heart leaps and I immediately know I'm seeing the future, but the future exists now! I am being *invited to go through the portal. I look at Diane, but then a woman screaming catches my attention. I notice the neighbors in the streets are starting to act strange and unpredictable. I am afraid again. The same woman who was screaming is now approaching me and grabbing both my hands. She looks like a zombie with blood pouring out of her eyes. I try to yank my hands free, but she's holding on too tightly. I start to panic. Then she starts making sounds. I panic more. She grips tighter. Then, it's as if earplugs are removed from my ears and I hear what she's saying.*

She's singing! The words to the song are something like:

"Let go of fear. We are strong together. We are love. We will create a world of love. We are free. We will create a free world together. We are all connected in love."

Before my eyes, her face becomes radiant and beautiful. Her eyes are clear and bright. She'd never been a zombie. It was my own fear that made me see her that way. She just awakened me!

My friend Diane is singing the song too and comes over to us. We all hold hands. I start singing with them, somehow knowing every word to this freedom song. Then everyone in the neighborhood joins us and we are one great chorus. Then I wake up.

This dream will forever be one of the most life-changing dreams I've ever had. Nothing has shown me more clearly how powerful the mind is, and that the choice to ascend into a future of love and harmony is fully my responsibility. When I am afraid, paranoid, and a victim, then that is the world I live in, choose, and create. When I am loving, kind, and visionary, then that is the future I'm participating in creating. It's that simple – for all of us.

Will we ascend into the positive polarity 4D Gaia, or repeat another 25,000 years in 3D?

What will it take for humanity to step out of confusion and into our eternal truth?

CHAPTER 18

CALLING TO OUR ALLIES FOR SUPPORT

The Higher Dimensional Helpers tell Duane and I that they are here for us, and all we need do is ask for support. Indeed, it has become quite common for us to see a shooting star or blazing "meteor" (AKA: multi-dimensional craft) streak the sky, after we put out a prayer of love to our helpers or a request for support. I'll never forget the emerald green ball of light with a bright red tail that flew out over the ocean in Tulum, Mexico as we sat with our students on the beach, having just requested the Arcturians' presence for a channeling. Wow! We feel them with us, protecting and guiding us, constantly.

In January 2019, just after the New Year crossing, there was a blood moon eclipse. Duane and I held a channeling session with the Higher Dimensional Helpers that night. Here is the transmission, which speaks to these times:

BIRTHING INTO FOURTH DENSITY

January 5, 2020

Council of Fifty Speaks on the Blood Moon Eclipse:

We Greet You in the Love of our Connected Intentions and in the Will of Divine Source:

Great transformation has happened many times. You must open your hearts to the destruction. To the dismantling. Love this, even in the time of explosions. Let it feel ecstatic. The breaking away of the old, disserving structures you've grown out of. There is always a pressure of the greatest fear and resistance right before a surrender into the ecstasy of re-generation. That is, you are going through a complete dismantling of the previous form to allow your consciousness to re-assimilate into the great Universal field and then birth again into your new form.

The mother cannot hold the child in her womb with any amount of will. For you see it is the moment of releasing personal will to divine will.

And trusting that this great universe/multiverse is intelligent beyond your wildest knowing.

We sooth your hearts now. For every stimulus, through all layers of reality, have but one purpose. To tickle you into letting go...

Letting go of perceiving any of it as personal.

Surrender is the alignment and complete harmonization of the will with the divine will. So, it is not a negating of personal will. The surrender is to the ego's control and belief that it is divine will. It is so easy to mistake the ego's desires and planning and prayers for divine will... No matter how dressed up in spiritual language and adornment, it is still your ego's agenda.

When it comes to death, there is nowhere else for the ego to go, but into its true form which is a particle of something much vaster. The ego will always resist dying.

And in your letting go, let the ego resist. Don't try to control your ego. Don't imagine that the ego will stand at attention to a higher power's instructions. Don't try to make yourself intimidating to the ego. It will not come into obeyance. This is basically just you splitting your ego into two factions and having a power game. In your power game, you project all manner of different faces onto the different parts of yourself vying for power. Take off all the faces and it's just you. You with you. You distracting you. You blocking you. You building stories.

You are not separate from the great birthing that is happening now. In this moment, open to the great nervous system of all of humanity. Feel the buzzing. The excitement. Feel the resistance of the ego. Feel the pressure for change. Now, expand yourself to know every planet's deepest desire. Journey into these celestial bodies... and experience their consciousness. Now you are not just human consciousness, but you are the consciousness of all forms of life, on and in, and around the planet. From this perspective everything is different. It is love that propels the transformation. It is a great dreaming that must manifest. It is a speeding towards the ecstasy of union.

The light of truth. The light of the One.

We are the Guardian Council of Earth,

...and we watch over this timeline... this co-dreamed timeline ... for all that you perceive, is a collaborative dreaming. An agreement of many, upon the creation of forms. And there is currently a very strong, and growing stronger, co-dreaming of transformation and a relief from delusion, deception, and lies.

Do you see, the internal processes of deception have reached their maximum fulfillment as a stimulus for growth? At this time, it is a choice toward love that will bring the next evolutionary leap. Up until now, you have been learning and growing from experiencing what you're not. You have dived in head first to roles of perpetrator, savior, and victim.

Now it is time to evolve based on who and what you are. It is no longer the deception that will catalyze change.

This is how it has been. But it has run its course, and the potency of this way of learning has faded.

The leap is coming and it's filled with a desire and a dreaming of relief from suffering and a choice for love. Put down your weapons. Violence is now perceived by the majority on the planet as unnecessary.

The next step is to internally validate this deep knowing that love is the propelling force toward freedom and not violence, war, and the power-over striving. This self-validation must grow within each person and move each person into active service. Up until recently, most people have been giving their power away to authority figures and believing the lies of your media streams, telling them that peace will come only if you fight for it. War must be waged to take out enemies who stop peace from happening. Your power has been given away. Yet, we repeat, the majority on the planet have now woken up to the truth that love is the way forward.

Therefore, today, when a voice of authority barks an order, or a lie is woven and spread throughout the media circuit, a growing number of people will discern: "Do I hop to attention and follow the orders of this voice, which is feeling more and more removed from me, less and less in service to me and my community, and more and more distant from the truth? Do I hop to attention and follow orders like I used to, or do I discern the truth within my heart and follow these deeper instructions?" Within each person this must happen and is happening and the tide is shifting, changing, turning more quickly every day.

No longer will people say "Yes, Sir." Now people will look into the eyes of their neighbors, all over the world, and only see the mirrored reflection back to them of: "We just want peace and love. Those instructions being barked, those orders, will not bring us together, but we can find the way together."

This great opening into the Fourth Density, feels like this. Do you feel it? In yourself, in your heart? It feels like this, a great leap of faith – that if you lay down your sword, the other in front of you with different colored skin or religious beliefs, will also lay down theirs. And then you will say, "Ahhhh, this whole time we've all been pawns in a great game. And the game masters have not had our highest good at heart. It has been a heart-less game. We liberate ourselves now from that bandwidth that has kept us asleep, into this ocean where everything is included and touched by the truth."

Each of you are deciding upon daily whether you desire to live in this ocean of peace and truth or whether you want to live in the discordant bandwidth of war, inner-battling, and fragmentation.

That's the only thing going on every day. And to think that there is something beyond this dictating life and reality is to feed the illusion, is to choose the inner-battle.

At this time, we bless you with the love pervasive in the universe. As we contact you – you contact us. We love you. You love us. We are one. We celebrate this sacred communion.

(End of Transmission)

CHAPTER 19

GOD IS EVERYTHING HAPPENING NOW

At one point in Book IV, Ra explains that The One is less involved in the act of "creation" and much more involved in knowing herself through her creation's diverse experiences! Meaning she isn't sitting apart from us, dreaming things into existence. She is Everything Happening Now. She is experiencing herself and coming to know herself through this Universe of Free Will. Free Will enables her to discover new areas of the consciousness that she is. Indeed, the catalyst of a negative polarity was one of these unexpected discoveries, Ra says.

We are the Creators of Reality,

living and breathing and dreaming, every day!

And not just we, humanity, but we all life on Earth, in our Solar System, in our Universe! Everything we be, see, touch, taste, hear, know, feel is the infinite intelligence of Intelligent Infinity stretching into new experiences.

Everything that makes us up – bacteria, fungus, parasites, yeasts, tiny micro-organisms that allow our human bodies and minds to function at peak performance; this is Creator's infinite intelligence creating endless connections within us. And when we share breath, electrons, fluids, love, thoughts, etc. with other living beings, that is the Creator linking all life in a great network of consciousness, her Consciousness. Everything is The One.

As human beings, our very thoughts, feelings, and intentions are our creation tools. We think up to 60,000 thoughts a day, every day. Ninety percent of these are repetitive thoughts cycling over and over again, reinforcing information and beliefs hardwired in us from the past. If we are awake in our True Selves, then we know we are Intelligent Infinity having an experience of finite reality and that our thoughts are the power of creation in the finite realms. Just remembering this, we now have the ability to liberate all that locked down energy and direct this potent thought-power towards liberating all life from 3D narratives and structures which cause great harm. We also are empowered to open more and more to our vastness, not limited even by thought.

As fourth density consciousness expands on Earth, and the veil continues dropping, we will have more and more opportunity to do just that. For now, let's be pre-emptive and take conscious steps towards becoming clear channels for the streams of Ascension Codes, full of information, pouring onto and into the Earth now.

Whether this planetary ascension is assisted by a solar event or another great flood, or we simply live out our current life serving to our highest ability, then die and birth into fourth density... I know whatever we face, we are ready for it. We have been preparing for 75,000 years. Perhaps this time around, we even have the wisdom to co-create our ascension as a blissful and graceful transition for all.

As we ascend from these reversal grids, the sun rises on a new day, a new world, and a new global destiny!

CHAPTER 20

WE ARE THE COUNCIL OF THE SUN

January 9, 2019

MARIA: He's opening a door. Bright golden light is streaming so fast through the door and the light penetrates everything instantaneously.

YESHUA SPEAKS: The concept of rules or "shoulds," protocols, or dogma does not fit for the Council of the Sun.

The purpose and mission lies within each of you, like a fire that cannot be put out. Your lives are guided by this light. Each person is a Universe of Wonders -magic and light. Opening the door illuminates the world. In this light, people see the truth when they look into the mirror, rather than the lies and the distortions.

This is the light of truth.

Opening the door should be your only care. Opening the door that the light comes in through.

The light is love.

No matter who they are or what they've been through doesn't matter. Love is the light streaming through that door. And if you are that light, when somebody is with you, they can suddenly feel who they truly are when they are in the light.

If you gather, do it because it brings you joy. When you gather, do this with each other: Open the door and mirror to each other the truth. This will help you to be strong enough to keep opening the door. Everybody be willing to see yourself for who you truly are. You'll be surprised who you truly are. There is nothing that cannot be transformed through true love.

True love cannot fully be transmitted unless the vessel becomes love itself.

There are plenty of people who I couldn't help. There are plenty who were suffering who I couldn't heal, because those were the moments I was in my contraction and afraid and in doubt.

The miracles that are recorded that have made it to present time for you to know about; the heart of these stories capture events that happened. These were moments I was able to surrender in entirety.

In those moments I was in so much love and clarity that all is love, that nothing else could exist. In those moments I did transcend time and space. My consciousness was of twelfth dimensionality.

It was because I was able to hold that frequency for the length of time needed for the person ailing to entrain completely to my frequency, and they had to be willing and say 'yes' to it and then healing happened. And it's irreversible.

It has been an ongoing agenda of the power-over paradigm to create as many obstacles as possible to people experiencing their divinity in its entirety.

Therefore, there always is a percentage of doubt that weakens the transmission.

Now I will bring through this frequency to you:

(Maria and Duane receive a flood of golden Love-Light into their bodies, minds and hearts.)

Let go of feelings of failure to save the illusion of this age. This age has come to an end. These are the times of ecstatic dying. Dying to who you were. Let the lies die.

Do not wait for or grasp for new technologies. Be...BE the technology awakening on the planet. Be the higher frequency. You are the greatest of all technology.

Humanity must know this. For you activate each other. You bring each other to your highest expressions.

(End of Transmission)

CHAPTER 21

PREPARING FOR ASCENSION

The catalysts for awakening are in rapid fire mode now. When you can perceive the upheavals, dramas, and craziness in our world all as opportunities or catalysts to wake you up, you step into empowerment in your life. Seeing through illusion is one thing. Living from your deepest core values is a whole other courageous act. Not many of us have this courage. Yet, this is what it will take to reclaim your fragments and become whole. What do I mean by this? Every one of us carries the truth within us, of who we really are and the greater consciousness we are a part of. Every moment of every day we face decisions to have our lives aligned with our truth, or misaligned with it. Every time you choose to live a life misaligned to your true nature, you fragment, and thus weaken yourself. The Harvest time you find yourself in now invites you to release all self-judgment for choices you regret in your past and show up 100% for a new choice today. Will you choose the positive polarity, service-to-others? Or negative polarity, service-to-self? Once you choose love over fear, the powerful resonance of that field will keep you on track. You will not be able to compromise yourself without feeling ill or soul-sick.

Supportive Suggestions

I realize I have just given you a lot of information. I highly recommend some intentional integration time. Come back to this book in a few days and read it through again. This offering is a meditation as much as it is a catalyst. The invitation for you is to discover a path forward from this moment that is your most authentic path.

Here are my supportive suggestions for you, as you shape a path through this Ascension time:

1. Do whatever you can to get MORE in your body. Meaning, do your inner-work of healing and transforming core wounds, so you can live securely in your body without dissociating. Belong to your body and astral body and tend to them lovingly. Balance your hormones. Exercise, eat clean, hydrate, detox, meditate!

2. If you are choosing to depart from body and personality at this time, you can choose for this to be your Ascension moment. Be willing to surrender all grasping of the ego to the material reality and personalities. Forgive and have compassion for all who have run amuck in the chaos, lost from center. Meditate on traveling into your center, where you become ultimate peace and love. You are your own

true portal into the eternal realms. Invoke your spiritual midwives to be close, to let you see them and feel them more clearly each day, each hour. Thank you for your service, precious Soul. It's time to go home.

3. For those in bodies, become a Clear Channel for your Soul's Light. Learn healthy boundaries with people and spirit-entities. Honor your body as a temple and a divine conduit for the Ascension Energies. Practice communing with the Quantum Field and shifting your brainwaves so that you're open to your infinite nature. Do breathwork to bring coherence to your heart field and strengthen your energy body, while relaxing your emotional and mental bodies.

4. Unplug from mainstream entertainment and media. Strengthen your Presence, rather than your personality. Give social media a break to re-estalish a sacred bond with yourself that exists without an audience. Have days where you are not online or on your phone. Turn your WiFi off when going to sleep. Connect deeply with nature for rejuvenation and healing.

5. Learn how to raise your vibration. Rise above the dense collective-consciousness bandwidths of fear, anxiety, depression, doubt, shame and anger. Many of these vibrations are being incited by mind-control technology. Listen to Whole Brain music, Solfeggio Scale tones, live crystal or Tibetan bowls, spiritual chants or songs or poetry, and uplifting stories. Spend time in the presence of advanced loving teachers – human and other than human.

6. Be in gratitude every day. It is the most clearing, liberating, healing and aligning energy frequency for your whole system!

...EXHALE

Dear Friends,

For those of you who have read this book all the way through to the end, I am grateful and honored to have been a temporary guide on a likely unexpected journey. I do not share my beliefs needing you to understand me or believe the same way yourself, but just to share what gives me hope, inspires me and deepens my own faith.

I truly believe we are entering into a Golden Age on Earth, where we will reclaim our lost histories, enter into the Galactic Family again, and re-discover our innate divinity.

Thank you for being You. Thank you for all that you are doing to protect the sacred timeline and support ascension. And thank you for receiving this outpouring of love from the Universe, through me. I look forward to creating our new beautiful world together!

With Love,
Maria Owl

RESOURCES

Messages from the Higher Dimensional Helpers through Maria Owl: https://soundcloud.com/user-964868314, https://www.youtube.com/channel/UCWkrmOLCxJujvOl8Qs TlRfw

The Law of ONE, Books One through Four, by Ra, an humble messenger of the Law of One. And the informational website and glossary: https://www.lawofone.info/. Credit to: www.llresearch.org

More on the work of Scott Mandelker: https://www.scottmandelker.com/

Learn more about the work of Gene Decode: www.GeneDecode.org

Finite-life grids and the "flower of death" pattern: Jere Rivera Dugenio research: https://nevodevelopment.com/dr-jere-rivera-dugenio/

The New New Testament: A Bible for the 21st Century, Edited by Hal Taussig, First Mariner Books, Boston, 2013

Link to Washington Post article on Palenque Ruins: https://www.washingtonpost.com/lifestyle/travel/mexicos-mysterious-mayan-ruins-at-palenque-now-accessible-from-the-air/2014/06/12/f71f7cb0-eda7-11e3-b84b-3393a45b80f1_story.html

Learn more about the work of Alex Collier, Andromendan Contactee: www.AlexCollier.org

Learn more about Tara and the Reverse Black Hole:
https://ascensionglossary.com/

More info on the Earth's magnetism weakening:
http://www.livescience.com/46694-magnetic-field-weakens.html

More on the Schumann Resonance information from Dr. Kathy J. Forti: https://trinfinity8.com/why-is-earths-schumann-resonance-accelerating/

Info on Solar Flash from David Wilcock & NASA:
https://divinecosmos.com/books-free-online/the-divine-cosmos/102-the-divine-cosmos-chapter-08-the-transformation-of-the-solar-system/

More on Samvartaka Fire:
https://en.wikipedia.org/wiki/S%C4%81%E1%B9%81vartaka

More on Solar Coronal Discharge event:
https://www.youtube.com/watch?v=GrnGi-q6iWc

Dr. Schavi M. Ali article on Sun Spots:
https://www.disclosurenews.it/en/major-cosmic-cleansing-on-the-horizon/

More info on "Cosmic Fluff" or the Photon Belt:
https://science.nasa.gov/science-news/science-at-nasa/2009/23dec_voyager/

Mayan Wisdom and Foundational Teachings - Casa Kin and Miguel Angel: https://casakin.org/

More on the Sun and Earth's magnetic relationship –
magnetic portals open to transfer the Sun's energy to Earth:

https://science.nasa.gov/science-news/science-at-nasa/2008/30oct_ftes/

Project Camelot interviews insider Bill Wood, ex-Navy Seal and senior Intuitive/Remote Viewer on Project Looking Glass. As of March, 2021, access was available here: https://www.youtube.com/watch?v=VtHCofbE1PM&list=PLq 9uLOwjoHHrPGh_P4815IJFC UbXdeOsv ,

...and also here: https://projectcamelotproductions.com/interviews/bill_wood/ bill_wood.html

Information on the Schumann Resonance with current reports: https://schumann-resonance.earth/

More from Laura Eisenhower: https://www.youtube.com/user/LauraEisenhower

ABOUT THE AUTHOR

Maria Christina Owl is the founder and CEO at Sacred Future. In her lightwork she supports men and women to deprogram reversal/inversion implants, heal and integrate their astral bodies from false timeline loops, and step into Fourth Density as whole, empowered and joyful. Maria works with private clients and groups around the globe, and hosts individuals and couples in Hawaii for private transformational retreats.

The Temple of Remembering was birthed by Maria Owl and Duane Vos in August of 2020. It is a beautiful land-based sanctuary dedicated to the awakening of healthy, sacred community through earth-based re-connection-focused ceremonies.

To learn more about Maria's lightwork mission and the work she and Duane are doing globally for humanity's highest timeline, go to www.sacredfuture.org.

Made in the USA
Las Vegas, NV
13 February 2022

43872551R00118